OECD ECONOMIC SURVEYS

NORWAY

ORGANISATION FOR ECONOMIC CO-OPERATION AND DEVELOPMENT

Pursuant to article 1 of the Convention signed in Paris on 14th December 1960, and which came into force on 30th September 1961, the Organisation for Economic Co-operation and Development (OECD) shall promote policies designed:

- to achieve the highest sustainable economic growth and employment and a rising standard of living in Member countries, while maintaining financial stability, and thus to contribute to the development of the world economy;
- to contribute to sound economic expansion in Member as well as non-member countries in the process of economic development; and
- to contribute to the expansion of world trade on a multilateral, non-discriminatory basis in accordance with international obligations.

The original Member countries of the OECD are Austria, Belgium, Canada, Denmark, France, the Federal Republic of Germany, Greece, Iceland, Ireland, Italy, Luxembourg, the Netherlands, Norway, Portugal, Spain, Sweden, Switzerland, Turkey, the United Kingdom and the United States. The following countries became Members subsequently through accession at the dates indicated hereafter: Japan (28th April 1964), Finland (28th January 1969), Australia (7th June 1971) and New Zealand (29th May 1973).

The Socialist Federal Republic of Yugoslavia takes part in some of the work of the OECD (agreement of 28th October 1961).

Publié également en français.

© OECD, 1989
Application for permission to reproduce or translate all or part of this publication should be made to:
Head of Publications Service, OECD
2, rue André-Pascal, 75775 PARIS CEDEX 16, France.

Table of contents

Introduction   9

I. The medium-term adjustment problem   10
    The oil-price collapse and corrective policy action   10
    Medium-term outlook and policy requirements   12

II. The policy setting   16
    Fiscal policy   16
    Monetary policy   21
    Incomes policy   25
    Supply-side policy   25

III. Recent trends and short-term prospects   28
    Overview   28
    Continued weakness of demand and output   30
    Pronounced pick-up in unemployment   33
    Progress on the inflation front   36
    Improving external position   38
    Short-term prospects and risks to the outlook   40

IV. The labour market and wage formation   45
    Labour market developments   45
    Wage increases and industry wage structure   49
    Institutions of wage determination   53
    Wage formation   59
    Summary   68

V. Conclusions   70

Notes and references   74

Annexes:
I. Theories of wage determination   75
II. Calendar of main economic events   81

Statistical annex   87

Tables

Text

1.	Terms-of-trade-induced losses in national income	11
2.	Net external debt	11
3.	The oil rent	14
4.	Budget balances: projections and outcome	17
5.	Actual and projected monetary growth	24
6.	Subsidies to the business sector	27
7.	The economy: projections and outcome	29
8.	Supply and use of resources	32
9.	Prices, wages and incomes	38
10.	Short-term prospects	41
11.	Current external account projections	43
12.	Labour market indicators	46
13.	The structure of unemployment	46
14.	Incidence of unemployment	47
15.	Hidden labour reserves	47
16.	Sectoral employment shares	48
17.	Trade union membership as a percentage of total labour force	54
18.	Trade union membership by sector and affiliation	54

Statistical annex

A.	Supply and use of resources, current prices	87
B.	Supply and use of resources	88
C.	Gross domestic product by origin, current prices	89
D.	Gross domestic product by origin	90
E.	General Government income and expenditure	91
F.	Production by sector	92

G.	Labour market and employment	93
H.	Balance of payments	94
I.	Foreign trade, total and by area	96
J.	Prices and wages	97
K.	Money and credit	98

Diagrams

1.	Local government net debt	18
2.	Fiscal indicators	20
3.	Interest rates and the exchange rate	22
4.	Financial balances	30
5.	Household saving and consumption	31
6.	Labour market developments	34
7.	Prices and costs by international comparison	37
8.	Current external account	39
9.	Wage increases and unemployment	50
10.	International competitiveness in manufacturing	51
11.	Occupational wage structure	52
12.	Centrally-determined wages and wagedrift	57

This Survey is based on the Secretariat's study prepared for the annual review of Norway by the Economic and Development Review Committee on 15th December 1988.

After revisions in the light of discussions during the review, final approval of the Survey for publication was given by the Committee on 17th January 1989.

The previous survey of Norway was issued in January 1988.

BASIC STATISTICS OF NORWAY

THE LAND

Area (1 000 sq. km) 1983	324	Major cities (1.1.88):	
Agricultural area (1 000 sq. km) 1983	9	Oslo	450 808
Productive forests (1 000 sq. km) 1983	65	Bergen	209 912

THE PEOPLE

Population (31.12.87)	4 198 637	Civilian employment, 1987	2 126 000
No. of inhabitants per sq. km	14	*of which:* Industry (%)	26.5
Net natural increase (average 1982-1987)	8 445	Agriculture, forestry and fishing (%)	6.5
Per 1 000 inhabitants (average 1982-1987)	2.0	Other activities (%)	67.0

PRODUCTION

Gross domestic product in 1987 (millions of Kr.)	556 924	Gross fixed capital formation (1987):	
GDP per head (US$)	19 678	Percentage of GDP	28.0
		Per head, US$	5 520

THE GOVERNMENT

Public consumption in 1987 (percentage of GDP)	20.9	Composition of Parliament (No. of seats):	
General government current and capital expenditure in 1987 (percentage of GDP)	49.5	Labour party	71
		Conservative party	50
General government current revenue in 1987 (percentage of GDP)	55.7	Christian democratic party	16
		Centre (Agrarian) party	12
		Progress party	2
		The socialist left party	6
		Total	157
Last general election: 1985		Next general election: September 1989	

FOREIGN TRADE

Exports of goods and services as a percentage of GDP (average 1983-1987)	48.5	Imports of goods and services as a percentage of GDP (average 1983-1987)	44.5
of which:		Main imports in 1987 (percentage of total commodity imports):	
Gross freight and oil drilling earnings (1983-1987)	7.8	Ships	1.0
Main exports in 1987 (percentage of total commodity exports):		Machinery, apparatus and transport equipment (excl. ships)	34.0
Forestry products	5.2	Raw materials (non-edible) incl. fuels and chemicals	13.1
Base metals and products thereof	13.8	Base metals and products thereof	9.3
Fish and fish products	6.6		
Machinery, apparatus and transport equipment (excl. ships)	9.3		

THE CURRENCY

Monetary unit: Krone	Currency units per US$, average of daily figures:	
	Year 1987	6.74
	November 1988	6.57

Note: An international comparison of certain basic statistics is given in an annex table.

Introduction

1988 marks the third year of adjustment to lower oil prices. Austerity policies pursued since the spring of 1986 have begun to affect the labour market, with unemployment being pushed up to high levels by Norwegian standards. As the inflation momentum stemming from the period of overheating in the mid-1980s was slow to abate, the Government imposed a one-year wage freeze in March 1988, giving in conjunction with a marked easing of domestic demand pressure a renewed downward twist to the deceleration of inflation. Restrictive economic policies and buoyant international demand combined to reduce the current external deficit, though it is still high by international comparison. Although the development of new oil fields will boost energy-export earnings, restoration of a satisfactory balance in the external economy remains a challenge to policy-making.

The Survey starts with a brief exposition of Norway's medium-term adjustment problem. After recapitulating developments which had thrown the economy off balance and reviewing stabilisation results achieved so far, issues relating to the further course of the rebalancing process are discussed in Part I. Medium-term scenarios indicate that moderation in public expenditure growth is essential. As shown in Part II, however, fiscal restraint has been mainly achieved so far through higher taxes; no change in the fiscal policy stance is planned for 1989. On present trends and policies, the unwinding of internal and external imbalances is therefore likely to continue, though at a slower pace than hitherto (Part III).

A prerequisite for continued external adjustment is sustained improvement in international competitiveness along with enhanced relative profitability in exposed non-oil industries. The tendency of labour costs to grow in excess of those in trading partner countries will have to be reversed and a shift of resources from the sheltered sectors of the economy will have to take place. Part IV of the Survey examines in some depth structural and behavioural labour market features and the wage formation process, with particular emphasis on the institutional setting. The main conclusions which can be drawn from the Survey are summarised in Part V, together with some policy considerations.

I. The medium-term adjustment problem

The oil-price collapse and corrective policy action

The oil-price collapse in 1985/86 implied a dramatic fall in Norway's real disposable income at a time when the economy was in an acute state of overheating. Within a year, the current account position swung from a surplus of 5½ per cent of GDP to a deficit of 6½ per cent. As evidenced by growing deficits of the Mainland economy, the underlying external position had already been weakening before, owing to the combination of strong domestic demand and real appreciation of the krone. Indeed, when oil revenue is spent in an economy operating at full employment, an import surplus in traditional goods and services can be expected as a natural outcome. The continued though diminishing effects of the oil income injection were compounded towards the mid-1980s by a sharp fall in the household saving ratio and strong growth in investment in both exposed and sheltered sectors, linked to financial market liberalisation and expectations of buoyant income growth in the future. The implications for the external account were masked, though, by high energy export revenues.

The oil-induced fall in real disposable income of 10 per cent of GDP was a much bigger supply shock than any OECD country had to face during either of the two oil-price hikes in the 1970s (Table 1). The growth of the oil sector had allowed Norway to maintain high spending and employment levels in the decade to the mid-1980s when most OECD countries suffered from relatively weak demand and rapidly-rising unemployment, and many of them from balance-of-payments difficulties as well. Increased domestic expenditure cushioned the Norwegian economy from the effects of temporary increases in world savings in the wake of the oil shocks in the 1970s. Also, since most of the oil revenue was appropriated by the Government, an enviable combination of strong public expenditure growth and rising budgetary surpluses emerged. Moreover, the Government could apparently afford to be more lenient towards inflation as the balance-of-payments consequences of higher relative costs than abroad could be compensated for by increased oil revenues. Indeed, during

Table 1. **Terms-of-trade-induced losses in national income**
Per cent of GDP

Norway	**1985-87**	**–10.6**
Japan	1973-75	–3.8
	1978-80	–5.4
OECD Europe	1973-75	–2.0
	1978-80	–1.6

Source: OECD, *Historical Statistics* 1960-86, Paris 1988.

the first half of the 1980s current account surpluses permitted a major reduction of the net foreign debt incurred during the early phases of oil development (Table 2). Even so, at its nadir in 1985 Norway's net external liability position against the rest of the world was just back to the level prior to the advent of oil income flows.

The oil-price collapse and the overheating in the domestic economy called for a swift policy reaction to prevent imbalances from widening, and for more fundamental policy changes to restore a healthy external balance over the medium term. The new Government, which took office in Spring 1986, set out a three-pronged strategy to restructure and rebalance the economy:

– Domestic demand was to be sharply curtailed in order to reduce pressures on resources and compress imports;

Table 2. **Net external debt**
Kr. billion

	1970	1975	1980	1985	1986
Total net external debt	9.1	35.2	93.0	48.7	80.5
Of which:					
Shipping sector	6.8	10.9	21.9	29.4	20.5
Oil activity	–	13.0	19.7	36.6	45.8
Mainland Norway	2.3	11.3	51.4	–17.3	14.2
Of which:					
Central Government	1.2	4.5	25.5	0.6	5.6
Memorandum item:					
Total net external debt, per cent of GDP	11	24	33	10	16

Source: *National Budget* 1989, Oslo 1988.

- Competitiveness of the exposed sector was to be improved in order to regain market shares both at home and abroad, and to cushion economic growth from the effects of domestic-demand compression;
- The supply-side of the economy was to be strengthened by measures to increase national savings and improving the efficiency of the economy.

In the event, domestic demand has been curtailed by tight fiscal and monetary policies, but despite a rather prompt 10 per cent devaluation, external competitiveness worsened further in 1986 and 1987, and major structural impediments have remained. Large cost increases, though decelerating more recently, have more than eroded the gains from the devaluation. With no improvement in cost-competitiveness and a weak profit position in parts of the exposed (non-oil) sector, the desired resource transfer from the sheltered sector has not yet begun. Manufacturing employment continued to shrink, while the sheltered sectors increased employment up to mid-1988. The authorities have made some moves in the field of structural and micro-policies. Industrial support has been reduced somewhat in recent years, but remains high in some sectors, notably agriculture. The most important initiative taken in the field of supply-side policies was the tax reform programme: first steps have been taken to stimulate efficiency through marginal tax rate reductions, and the distorting effects of tax deductibility of interest payments have been reduced.

Despite the deterioration in external competitiveness and only-limited improvements on the supply side, there has been a marked reduction in the underlying external imbalance. As oil revenue fell, the improvement in the current account can be ascribed to both demand compression in the Mainland economy and an unexpectedly buoyant world economy. Demand compression has reduced imports directly, but it may also have improved the external balance by encouraging exports. The ease with which the economy has absorbed expenditure cuts without a marked reduction in Mainland output and sharp increases in unemployment is due to the fact that spending cuts were concentrated on imported goods. Impressive though the reduction in the external imbalance has been, its complete elimination, let alone its eventual replacement by a surplus, still faces the economy with a sizeable adjustment problem.

Medium-term outlook and policy requirements

As to the continuation of the rebalancing process, two sets of questions may be raised. *First*, what is the appropriate target for the current account, and to what extent should it be made dependent on oil sector activities and oil prices? *Secondly*, how fast should the economy approach any given target and what means should be used to attain it?

Experience from other Member countries suggests that Norway might be able to run large current-account deficits over the medium term without facing serious financing problems. However, this would impose a burden on future generations, which would have to service the ensuing external debt. A fast improvement in current account balance would yield benefits in terms of lower external debt and thus lower the servicing burden for future generations. This must, however, be balanced against the costs in terms of lost output and employment which would result from rapid adjustment. So far, the adjustment has relied largely on demand compression. To sustain the adjustment process and to bring about a lasting improvement in the external account, a major improvement in international competitiveness is required.

A dominant feature of the long-term economic outlook is that oil reserves in fields, which have been approved for development, may be depleted in the foreseeable future. Proven recoverable oil reserves are estimated to be about 1 750 million tons (about 13 billion barrels), compared to already-extracted oil of about 400 million tons (by the end of 1988). Should no new deposits be discovered, and recent explorations give no grounds for optimism in this respect, the volume of oil production will start falling in the latter part of the 1990s. Significant gas reserves have, however, been discovered on the Continental Shelf. At present production levels, these reserves would last for about a century. But there are serious doubts about the extent to which increased gas production can replace oil as a sustained source of national income. The cost of extraction will be high in most fields, and bringing gas to the consumer will be costly. Barring major price rises and a technological breakthrough in gas transportation, high production levels in the petroleum sector cannot be expected to be maintained beyond the turn of the century.

This raises important issues regarding income distribution between generations in the "oil period" and the post-oil era. As long as petroleum prices exceed extraction costs, the economy derives a windfall gain. Though the rental element in petroleum prices has been reduced substantially since the 1985/86 collapse, it was still sizeable in 1987 (Table 3). If rents associated with oil production are consumed as fast as they accrue, this would be at the cost of future income. Future generations would not only be without any benefit from the oil wealth but would also have to step up investment to rebuild and to expand the non-oil economy. The reverse would hold if all of the oil rents were saved. Oil extraction would in this case only involve asset substitution, and

Table 3. **The oil rent**[1]
Per cent of GDP

1977	1½
1978	3
1979	5½
1980	11
1981	11
1982	10½
1983	12
1984	13
1985	12½
1986	3½
1987	3

1. The oil rent is the difference between oil revenues and production costs, where the rate of return on capital is taken to be equal to the average rate of return in manufacturing.

Source: Norges Offentlige Utredninger, *Norsk okonomi i forandring. Perspektiver for nasjonalformue og okonomisk politikk i 1990-arene*, (NOU 1988:21), Oslo 1988.

the current generation would not be reaping any gains from the oil wealth. It would appear that the most appropriate solution to the intertemporal/intergenerational distribution problem is to keep oil production down to reasonable levels and to share the windfall of current production between the present and the future by saving part of the accrued oil rent. This would be a departure from the current situation where debt is incurred with negative implications for future disposable income.

In the present state of the oil market, retaining oil in the ground would seem to offer high potential rates of return. However, this option is not only risky but also difficult to implement for both technical and political reasons. Investing oil money in productive capital at home would also seem unattractive on present low rates of return on fixed investment relative to other assets and in view of the difficulty in designing incentive schemes to induce extra capital spending. Investment in infrastructure and human capital might offer possibilities to transfer economically and socially useful wealth to post-oil generations but the benefits of such investment cannot be evenly spread and the selection process would be difficult. Furthermore – and this holds for all forms of oil-money spending at home – this would add to already high pressure on resources and would thus run counter to the required improvement of the external non-oil current balance. On these considerations, building up an asset position against the rest of the world would seem to be the most promising option. Apart from offering a relatively safe and profitable source of income, such an approach would cushion the production structure from the disruptive effects of the eventual termination of oil export revenues. The higher the net interest income flow from abroad and the greater the possibilities to run down (excessive) foreign exchange reserves, the less the burden on the production apparatus to increase its export-revenue-generating capacity.

In order to attain current-account surpluses, a major improvement in competitiveness is required, as well as increased national savings. On the basis of present policy trends, this does not seem likely without recourse to higher oil exports. Under the impact of public expenditure growth and buoyant investment in the oil sector, aggregate demand growth is set to pick up. After the oil-price collapse, investment activity was expected to fall steeply in the medium term. In sharp contrast to this pessimism, oil companies became more bullish on capital spending in the course of 1987, spurred by tax changes, better cost control and a firming of oil prices. Despite the authorities' intentions to limit investment activity in the oil sector, on the basis of decisions already taken, an investment boom is likely to occur in the early 1990s.

In view of the considerations outlined above, this would strongly argue for moderation in public expenditure growth. Existing commitments in the field of social security will, however, put strong upward pressure on public spending, as discussed in last year's Annual Survey. The ageing of the population is expected to increase the number of retired people by 11 per cent in the 1985-1995 period. The impact on pension outlays will be compounded by the maturing of the pension system, with standard pensions foreseen to rise at an average annual rate of 2 to 3 per cent in real terms between 1985 and 1995. Government commitments in other areas, such as health care and defence, will also put upward pressure on public expenditure. A recent estimate by the Ministry of Finance shows that the automaticity in public spending could keep total outlays growing at an average real annual rate of 2 per cent up to 1995. Given prospective increases of a discretionary nature, this figure may considerably understate the build-up of pressure for higher public expenditure. The desired deceleration of public expenditure growth should mainly be attained by reducing growth in transfers and scaling-back subsidies to agriculture and other industries.

II. The policy setting

As noted above, the Government's medium-term economic strategy to restore external balance is aimed at curbing domestic demand through restrictive macroeconomic policies so as to reduce inflationary pressures and create room for the expansion of the exposed sector, and enhancing the economy's growth potential by promoting restructuring and efficiency. Fiscal restraint was again exercised in 1988 but, with public expenditure projected to rise markedly in relation to GDP, no further tightening is envisaged for 1989. High interest rates, while contributing to exchange-rate stability, have led to a marked deceleration in credit expansion. Meeting the announced credit target for 1989 will require continued tight monetary conditions. The Government intervened in the income-formation process by regulating the growth of wages and dividends until March 1989. In the area of supply-side policies there were some further moves to liberate financial markets, reform the tax system and restructure state-owned companies.

Fiscal policy

The *1988 National Budget*, submitted to Parliament in October 1987, aimed at maintaining a tight fiscal stance for the third consecutive year, primarily through revenue-raising measures. A broadening of the tax base outweighed cuts in (high) marginal tax rates. Government expenditure, excluding spending related to oil activity, was projected to grow by some 2 per cent in volume. The *Revised National Budget*, presented in May 1988, included some rise in state bank lending quotas in connection with the spring collective wage settlements and a small extra appropriation for labour market measures. Adjustments to the original budget projections mainly reflected lower estimated oil revenues and increased expenditure on oil activities. Moreover, revisions took account of an apparent shortfall in tax revenues and net interest income.

Contrary to developments in 1987 when the reduction of tax arrears contributed to a better-than-expected outcome, the 1988 *central* government surplus is expected to turn out smaller than projected in the National Budget, dropping markedly from the year before (Table 4). To a large extent this is attributable to lower oil prices which reduced tax and royalty receipts and depressed profits from government participations in oil fields. Adjusted for these items and transfers from the Bank of Norway, the undershoot in the budget surplus was small and largely reflected a less favourable than estimated outcome for the previous year. Despite some shortfalls in indirect taxes and overruns in transfers associated with lower economic activity, the *rate of growth* of both total revenue and expenditure, excluding oil, appears to have been much as expected. Nonetheless, 1988 seems to have seen a turnaround in the oil-adjusted central government budget balance, which started moving back into deficit (Table 4), following a continued improvement since the middle of the 1980s.

The negative swing in the financial position of *general* government was even more pronounced (Table 4), as municipal debt kept rising rapidly. The strong growth in local government spending and employment has increased pressures in the economy, hampering a rechannelling of resources to exposed sectors. Given the sharp

Table 4. **Budget balances: projections and outcome**

	1987		1988		1989
	NB 87	Outcome	NB 88	Outcome	NB 89
	Per cent of GDP				
Surplus before loan transactions:					
Central government[1]	0.4	2.4	3.7	1.4	1.4
(administrative basis)	(0.0)	(1.5)	(1.6)	(0.4)	(0.8)
General government	−0.2	1.3	2.8	0.1	0.5
	Per cent of Mainland GDP				
Adjusted for oil activities and transfers from the Bank of Norway:					
Central government[1]	0.9	1.8	2.2	0.7	−0.5
(administrative basis)	(−0.7)	(0.1)	(−0.1)	(−0.4)	(−1.3)
General government	0.3	0.6	1.3	−0.6	−1.4
	Per cent of GDP				
General government net lending	0.2	3.9	5.0	2.3	1.8

1. Including social security.
Source: *National Budget* (NB), 1987, 1988, 1989.

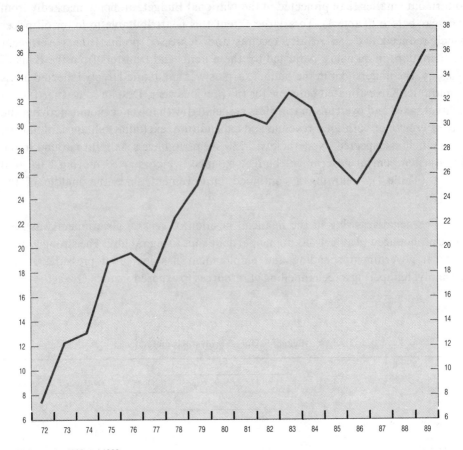

Diagram 1. **LOCAL GOVERNMENT NET DEBT**
Per cent of total revenue[1]

1. Estimates for 1988 and 1989.
Sources: Central Bureau of Statistics and Ministry of Finance.

increase in net debt of municipalities in relation to total revenue since 1986 (Diagram 1), the scope for increases in expenditure should become more limited. Indeed, there are indications of a slowdown in municipal investment in recent months. In the past, local authority expenditure persistently grew in excess of official projections. The Government has announced a reassessment of the situation in the local government sector and of the premises on which economic planning for lower levels of government rests. For improving control over municipal spending, stricter supervision of borrowing would seem necessary; but it would also seem important to curb the growth of revenue, which has tended to exceed official projections by wide margins and encouraged extra spending. Through its control over maximum rates of local income tax and its transfers to local authorities, the Central government has at its disposal powerful instruments for influencing the revenue of local authorities.

The *1989 National Budget* tries to reconcile conflicting policy goals: it aims at further reducing persisting large imbalances in the economy without jeopardising high employment levels. Excluding oil-related transactions and transfers from the Bank of Norway, the central government deficit before loan transactions is projected to rise by about 1 percentage point to 1¼ per cent of Mainland GDP (1/2 per cent in national accounts definition, Table 4). Non-oil revenues are expected to rise in relation to nominal GDP. Tax policy is being geared to assisting wage moderation: marginal tax rates on gross income are to be raised somewhat for high-income earners and reduced a little for lower income brackets. Indirect taxes and excise duties will be adjusted to give, on average, an increase in line with the expected inflation rate. Expenditure, excluding oil activity, is projected to grow 2 percentage points more than revenue; adjusted for special factors this means an expansion of over 3 per cent in real terms. The faster growth in general government spending mainly reflects steeply rising transfers, in particular to social security. Funds available for labour market measures will be increased by two-thirds compared with 1988 and a further rise in state bank lending has been budgeted after a sharp increase in 1988. The overall central government balance is officially projected to remain in surplus in 1989 (Table 4).

In order to assess the stance of fiscal policy, allowance must be made for automatic budget stabilizers. The pronounced economic downturn has resulted in lower tax receipts and higher payments for unemployment benefits. Adjusted for the cyclical weakening of the financial position, and net of interest payments, the non-oil *central* government budget balance is officially estimated to have improved further in 1988, though less than during the preceding two years (Diagram 2). The 1989 Budget implies an unchanged fiscal stance at the central government level.

Local government activities have tended to reduce the restrictive thrust of fiscal policy over the past two years. OECD estimates suggest that, after adjusting for changes in oil revenues, the improvement in the structural balance of *general* government may have amounted to around ½ per cent of GDP in both 1987 and 1988. On the official assumption of a drop in the local government deficit, this trend could continue in 1989; yet, as recognised in the National Budget, the outlook for municipal expenditure is highly uncertain.

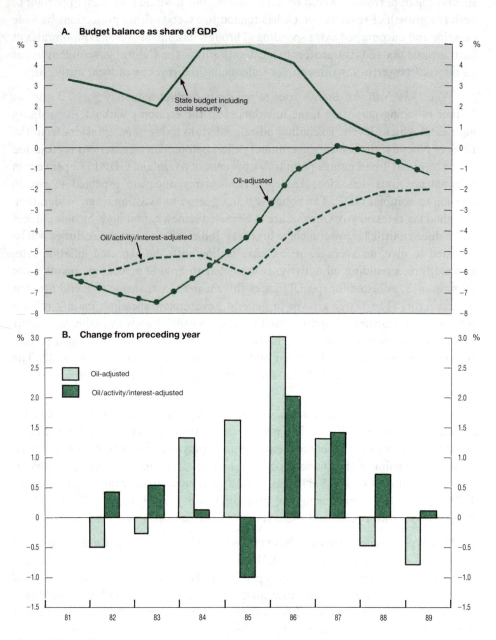

Diagram 2. **FISCAL INDICATORS**

Source: Ministry of Finance.

Monetary policy

Since 1986, the prime target of monetary policy has been the defence of the exchange rate and foreign exchange reserves: high interest rates have served to secure a net capital inflow to the private sector sufficient to match the current-account deficit and to keep the effective exchange rate broadly stable. The latter is measured by a (double-weighted) basket index including 14 currencies, with a swing margin of 2.25 per cent on either side of its central value. Changing market sentiment, mainly reflecting oil-price developments and concerns about inflationary trends has led to considerable, and sometimes abrupt, fluctuations within this band. When the exchange rate approached the ceiling of the target zone in mid-1987 (Diagram 3), the authorities decided to intervene in the foreign exchange market rather than to lower interest rates. Similarly, at the end of 1987, heavy intervention in support of the krone prevented the exchange rate from dropping out of the target range. When, in mid-1988, the krone again drifted towards the upper limit of the swing margin, exchange-market intervention was relatively limited and interest rates were lowered. This caused the exchange rate to weaken; but, helped by some sales of foreign currency, it has been kept safely within the target zone, despite depressed oil prices and higher international interest rates.

Exchange-rate management limits the scope for interest rates to be varied in response to domestic considerations. This constraint varies with market perception about the appropriateness of economic policies. In response to the weakening trend in domestic demand and the related marked easing of credit expansion, the central bank lowered its overnight lending rate in two stages in May and June 1988 by altogether 1 percentage point. There was a parallel decline in other money market rates. The decrease in bond rates was more limited (Diagram 3), resulting in a further flattening of the downward sloping yield curve. With the international level of interest rates firming, the gap between Norwegian and foreign rates, though remaining substantial, narrowed significantly. Long-term rates rebounded, however, in August and September. Short-term money market rates firmed, too, as official intervention in support of the currency led to a squeeze on liquidity. With little downward pressure on the krone in the aftermath of the presentation of the 1989 Budget and some easing of market interest rates, the central bank cut its overnight lending rate by another 0.4 percentage point to 12.4 per cent in late October. This was followed by renewed downward pressure on the exchange rate in mid-November. After sizeable central bank interventions and sharp increases in market interest rates, the krone strengthened again, and at the beginning of December the central bank lowered its overnight lending rate to 12 per cent, the lowest level since 1981. This brought down

Diagram 3. **INTEREST RATES AND THE EXCHANGE RATE**

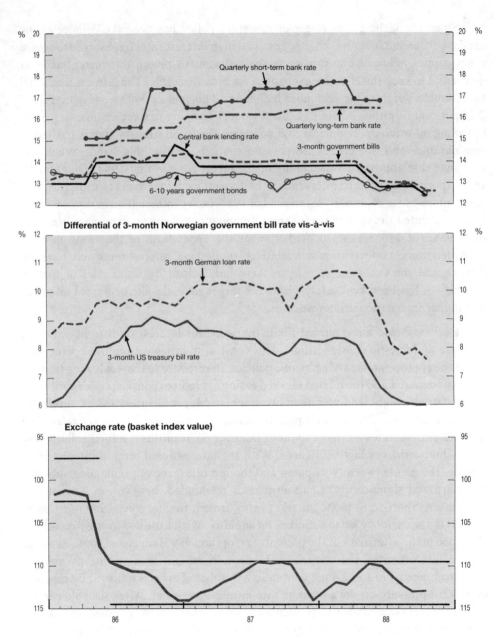

Source: Bank of Norway.

the interest rate differential against major trading partners to about 3 per cent, from about 8 per cent at the beginning of 1988.

High interest rates on housing loans continued to be of great concern to the authorities. Measures in the 1987 and 1988 Budgets have led to an increase in post-tax interest rates, adding to the debt-servicing burden of the heavily-indebted household sector. In connection with the spring 1988 income settlement, the Government requested banks to reduce interest rates on special home loans by 1 percentage point. A new special borrowing facility at the central bank compensates banks for the resulting income loss. Bank lending rates for other borrowers followed only hesitantly the reduction in money market rates, notwithstanding the abolition of reserve requirements and other measures to reduce bank lending rates relative to money market and bond market rates. At 16.5 per cent on average in the third quarter of 1988, they were down by ½ percentage point from their peak in the first quarter but still higher than two years ago, when money market rates peaked (Diagram 3). This reflects in part higher funding costs as a result of increased central bank financing and financing from abroad. Moreover, sharply-reduced profitability as a result of large losses on loans and securities has forced banks to seek higher income from traditional credit mediation. Commercial banks' losses on loans and guarantees in 1987 are now put at 1½ per cent of total advances, as compared with a long-term average of less than ½ per cent. On present indications, losses for 1988 could be at least as heavy as in 1987. Loan losses have most hit the wholesale and retail trade sector, and a few "growth industries", such as data processing and fish-farming.

Monetary growth has decelerated sharply (Table 5). With the contractionary influence of the government and the foreign sector diminishing, this reflects the marked slowdown in domestic credit expansion. Indeed, after persistently overshooting official targets and rising at rates of around 20 per cent in the mid-1980s, domestic credit seems set to meet the Budget objective of 8 to 12 per cent growth in 1988. Both supply- and demand-side factors contributed to this development. Banks' and financial institutions' losses, and their need for more equity capital, have led to stricter assessment of customers' creditworthiness and more frequent refusal of loan applications. The tightening of monetary policy and changes in the tax system have resulted in positive after-tax interest rates even for borrowers with the highest marginal tax rates. Together with the damping effect of fiscal policy this has contributed to lower demand for credit. Moreover, following the strong build-up in gross debt in the wake of credit market deregulation, the private sector appears to have completed the level adjustment of its financial assets. Other factors, which may explain the conspicuous slowdown in the accumulation of private and municipal

Table 5. **Actual and projected monetary growth**[1]
Contributions to growth in M2, in per cent

	1984	1985	1986	1987	1988	1989
Supply from Central Government sectors	5.5	2.3	2.3	−2.3	1.4	1.7
Through deficit before loan transactions	6.0	3.3	1.2	−6.4	−2.9	−2.8
Central Government loan transactions and the State Banks	−0.5	−1.0	1.1	4.0	4.3	4.5
Supply from private banks and the bond market	13.7	20.1	17.6	25.0	7.5	4.1
Supply from domestic sources	19.2	22.4	19.9	22.7	8.9	5.8
Supply through sales of foreign currency[2]	0.6	−7.4	−15.3	−6.6	−3.9	−0.8
Increase in non-bank liquidity (M2)	19.8	15.0	4.6	16.1	5.0	5.0
Memorandum items:						
Increase in credit indicator (end-year)	16.9	21.9	17.9	20.2	12	9
Nominal GDP growth (Mainland)	10.2	11.9	13.5	10.1	6.8	3.5

1. Excluding oil tax revenues, net interest payments and transfers to abroad.
2. Includes statistical discrepancies.
Source: Ministry of Finance.

financial assets in 1988, are the decline of activity in the stock and the housing markets, and the deceleration in inflation, permitting the level of real financial assets to be maintained at lower nominal growth.

According to the 1989 National Budget, domestic credit growth is intended to be kept within a 5 to 9 per cent range, which would represent a further significant deceleration. The government's borrowing abroad is planned to remain limited, implying that the current-account deficit should largely be financed by foreign loans to the commercial sector. The external deficit and capital outflow from other sectors have been mainly financed by short-term capital inflows to banks. The high level of non-residents' krone assets in the forward market and krone deposits with Norwegian banks, which developed in 1987, is a matter of some concern, as it constitutes a potential source for rapid and substantial capital outflows, as evidenced by the most recent unrest in financial markets. In order to increase stable long-term financing of the current account deficit, the commercial sector has been given greater scope to raise foreign currency loans: the changes proposed in the Budget include permission for sheltered industries to raise foreign currency loans and the removal of the ceiling on long-term foreign currency borrowing by enterprises. The authorities have, however, maintained restrictions on the purchase of Norwegian bonds by non-residents and on inward direct investment.

Incomes policy

The authorities have given incomes policy a central role in bringing domestic cost increases into line with developments abroad. In the 1987 wage bargaining round, Government measures contributed to zero settlements between the main union and employers' federations (LO and NAF) but wagedrift continued virtually unabated. The 1988 income settlement between LO and NAF was concluded after the Government accepted to take a number of measures in exchange for an agreement, which would limit *total* wage increases in 1988 to below 5 per cent, and offered prospects for continued wage moderation in 1989. The measures included greater availability of housing loans, lowering of mortgage interest rates, an extension of maternity leave, and early-retirement provisions. The latter two measures were to be implemented in the course of 1989 and 1990. The LO/NAF agreement was immediately followed by a decree, freezing wages and dividend payments. This was later replaced by an Income Regulation Act, which effectively imposed the LO/NAF agreement on all wage earners. As permissible wage increases were limited to 1 krone per hour, except for the low-paid and groups with low settlements in 1987, the percentage change was generally lower outside the LO/NAF area, where average incomes are higher. The Act defined income very broadly, thus minimising the possibility of evasion through income in kind and fringe benefits. The Act also limited dividend payments.

The Income Regulation Act has been successful in moderating wage increase in 1988 but the final verdict on this measure must be reserved for 1989, when the Act expires. The termination of the wage freeze period in the late-1970s was followed by a sharp acceleration in wage growth but this may have been due to factors other than pent-up pressure on wages (see Part IV). The weakening of the labour market during the period covered by the Act increases the chances of more lasting sustained effects on wages. An unwanted side-effect of the Act is the rigidity it introduces into the wage structure. This weakens the resource-allocative role of the wage system if prolonged over time. For 1989, the Government will continue to give incomes policy a prominent role. Details have yet to be worked out with the social partners, though the tax programme in the 1989 Budget may partly be seen as an incomes policy measure (see above).

Supply-side policy

Measures taken or under active consideration to improve the functioning of markets include:

- *Labour markets.* As noted, the number of places on special labour-market schemes has been increased considerably. Labour-market measures involve vocational training and work experience in both public and private educational establishments, thus leading to a better qualified workforce. They are principally targeted at youths in the age group 16-19, and should reduce the high incidence of unemployment among young people (see Part IV);
- *Financial markets.* A new legal framework for the functioning of the financial system was adopted in 1988, strengthening competitive forces in the market and bringing capital adequacy ratios more in line with those abroad. In July 1988, remaining quantitative restrictions on credit flows from non-bank financial institutions were abolished, as well as on borrowing in the bond market by credit institutions for housing purposes. As from December 1988, the Government eased restrictions on long-term borrowing in foreign currency by businesses, intended to increase the proportion of long-term capital inflows in the financing of the current-account deficit. With the aim of increasing risk capital available to the business sector, the Government has suspended the turnover tax on shares in 1989 and has also proposed simplification of the rules concerning foreign companies' purchases of property and stocks in Norway. Moreover, the Government will participate in a new venture capital company as a minority (49 per cent) shareholder.
- *Product markets.* Although budget support to industry has been curtailed in recent years, it remains very high for some sectors, especially agriculture (Table 6). This was discussed in some detail in the 1987 Survey. Subsidies were reduced somewhat in 1988, and the 1989 Budget proposal continues the regression. The authorities have announced that they will work towards a more efficient hydroelectric power market. This may involve greater harmonization of electricity prices across different users. The 1989 Budget calls for the abolition of differential excise duties on hydro-electric power. The restructuring of government-incorporated companies continued in 1988, with the aim of making them more responsive to competitive pressures;
- *Corporate tax reform.* The authorities are preparing changes in the corporate tax system to discourage tax-motivated investment by harmonising taxation of various forms of capital incomes and by broadening the tax base in order to create room for a reduction of statutory rates.
- *Personal tax reform.* The Government tax reform programme, discussed in

the 1987 Survey, has been aimed at reducing high statutory marginal tax rates and widening the tax base. The second stage of the programme was implemented in 1988 and the tax measures incorporated in the 1989 Budget complete the reforms.

Table 6. **Subsidies to the business sector**
Kr. million at 1987 prices

	1980	1981	1982	1983	1984	1985	1986	1987
Agriculture	9 566	10 995	11 227	11 134	11 160	11 141	10 242	10 079
Fishing	2 082	2 217	1 463	1 350	1 535	1 469	1 474	1 005
Manufacturing	4 285	5 669	8 154	6 201	6 199	4 651	6 462	4 690
Of which:								
Shipbuilding	1 127	1 742	1 397	922	718	898	1 029	979
State companies[1]	768	1 339	2 994	1 588	2 794	1 333	1 881	1 031
Guarantees to shipbuilding and oil drilling	–	1 700	691	77	38	40	–61	–
Private services	183	179	172	200	235	219	227	201
Other support	62	48	74	58	48	38	38	151
Total	16 178	20 808	21 781	19 020	19 215	17 557	18 382	16 125

1. Companies with more than 75 per cent government ownership. The amounts do not include the support state-owned companies have received through general support arrangements.
Source: National Budget 1989.

In order to support oil prices, the Government has continued to limit the increase in the supply of oil to international markets. The restrictions have reduced output by 7.5 per cent of capacity. It is yet to be decided whether the limitations will be extended beyond mid-1989.

III. Recent trends and short-term prospects

Overview

In 1988, under the impact of tight economic policies, real domestic demand declined for the second consecutive year. With both traditional exports and oil production rising strongly, total output seems to have kept growing at a modest pace while the virtual stagnation of the Mainland economy since mid-1986 appears to have continued. Yet, as can be seen from Table 7, national accounts data are subject to substantial revisions, and given the importance of activities related to oil and shipping, estimates of volume changes heavily depend on the price base used. Currently available information suggests that economic activity in 1987 was noticeably weaker than thought when Norway was examined a year ago, mainly as a result of the overestimation of non-oil investment. Notwithstanding a certain downward risk, overall activity in 1988 would seem to have developed much as foreshadowed in last year's Survey, with lower-than projected domestic demand, in particular private consumption and housing investment, largely compensated for by unexpectedly buoyant foreign demand.

A puzzling feature of developments in 1987 was the apparent decoupling of goods and labour markets: in spite of sharply lower output growth, labour market conditions kept tightening. This changed abruptly in 1988 when unemployment began to rise unexpectedly sharply (Table 7). With labour markets still very tight at the time of the spring wage round, a statutory wage freeze was imposed, which has helped avoid a major overshooting of the official inflation target. The easing of labour market pressures should contribute to prevent wage inflation from accelerating when the present income regulation expires in Spring 1989, which should bring price increases into line with those in trading partner countries.

Despite a marked deterioration in the terms of trade, the favourable trend in the real foreign balance has led to a better outcome for the current account in 1988 than expected a year ago. The fall in the external deficit since 1986 has been mirrored by a

Table 7. **The economy: projections and outcome**
Percentage change, volume

	1987				1988			
	NB 88[1]	OECD 87/88[2]	NB 89[3]	OECD 88/89[4]	NB 88[1]	OECD 88/89[2]	NB 89[3]	OECD 88/89[4]
Domestic demand	–0.8	–1½	–2.0	–3.4	1.2	½	–1.1	–1
Private consumption	–2.0	–2½	–2.2	–2.2	–1.7	–2¼	–2.5	–2½
Public consumption	2.2	–2¼	3.7	3.7	0.0	1	–0.1	¾
Fixed investment	0.1	–2½	–2.4	–7.9	4.5	5¾	5.0	4½
Stockbuilding[5]	–0.3	0	–0.9	–0.8	0.9	0	–1.0	–1
Exports	3.2	3½	0.3	2.0	0.5	¾	2.6	2¾
Imports	–2.8	–3	–6.7	–6.8	0.8	0	–2.3	–1¼
Foreign balance[5]	2.3	3	2.8	3.7	0.0	½	1.7	1¾
GDP	1.5	1¾	0.9	0.5	1.1	1	0.7	1
Mainland GDP	0.9	1	0.2	0.0	0.4	0	–0.2	0
Employment	0.4[6]	2	0.0[6]	1.9	–0.6[6]	½	–0.9[6]	–¾
Unemployment rate	..	2¼		2.1	..	2½	..	3
Consumer price deflator	8½[7]	8½	8.7[7]	8.1	5.0[7]	6¼	6½[7]	5¾
Current external balance (per cent of GDP)	–5.6	–5½	5.0	5.0	6.0	5½	4.3	3¾

1. 1986 prices.
2. 1980 prices.
3. 1987 prices.
4. 1984 prices.
5. Change as a percentage of GDP in previous period.
6. Man-years.
7. Consumer price index.

Sources: *National Budgets (NB)* 1988 and 1989; OECD *Economic Surveys*, Norway (OECD 87/88 and OECD 88/89).

downward adjustment of investment relative to national disposable income rather than a rise in the national saving ratio. Household sector dissaving has slowed but at the same time public sector saving has declined despite fiscal tightening. As public investment has kept rising, this has resulted in a marked reduction in the government's financial surplus, partly offsetting the fall in the private sectors' financial deficit (Diagram 4). Net borrowing by enterprises has fallen back to levels observed in the first half of the 1980s, with the decline in Mainland investment only partly offset by higher investment in oil and shipping. With private consumption falling and residential investment stagnating in real terms, the household sector's net debt accumulation has also slowed down markedly, though remaining extraordinarily high by historical standards. The size of the private sector's financial deficit, about 6 per cent of GDP in 1988, illustrates the adjustment problem the economy is still facing. On present policies, domestic demand is projected by the Secretariat to remain weak in the near term but to stop falling thereafter. This would seem to allow a continued gradual unwinding of imbalances but leave the economy with an external deficit in 1989 and 1990.

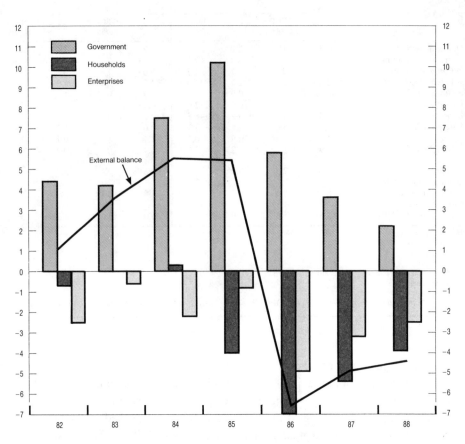

Diagram 4. **FINANCIAL BALANCES**
Per cent of GDP

Sources: Ministry of Finance; Bank of Norway; OECD estimates.

Continued weakness of demand and output

Private consumption has declined in volume since mid-1986 but still exceeds the 1984 level by about 11 per cent. According to revised data, household current expenditure exceeded disposable income by almost 7½ per cent in 1986, pushing the household sector into a net debtor position. This trend was clearly not sustainable, all the more so as higher interest rates raised the debt servicing burden while income

Diagram 5. **HOUSEHOLD SAVING AND CONSUMPTION**

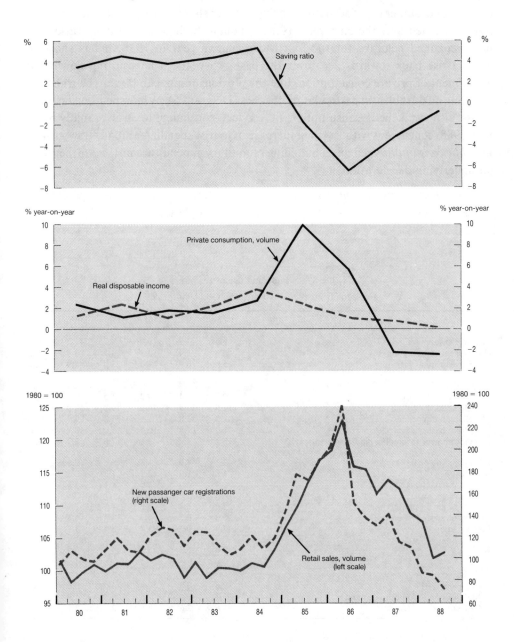

Sources: Central Bureau of Statistics and OECD.

growth decelerated and income expectations became more uncertain. Positive wealth effects on consumer demand stemming from higher share and especially house prices have weakened over the past year. Hence, though the household saving ratio may have remained negative for the fourth consecutive year in 1988, it has shown a distinct rise back towards zero over the past two years. The resulting downward adjustment of private consumption, like the previous jump, can largely be traced to spending on durables, in particular motor cars (Diagram 5). While spending on other goods also weakened, consumption of services continued to grow rapidly until mid-1988, concurrent with a strong increase in tourist spending abroad. Low growth in *public consumption* reflects a bunching of military expenditure in 1987 rather then an underlying deceleration.

Residential investment has displayed a pattern similar to that of current household demand (Table 8) but, given the usual completion lags, the adjustment of

Table 8. **Supply and use of resources**

Per cent from previous year, volume (1984 prices)

	1983	1984	1985	1986	1987	1988[2]
Private consumption	1.5	2.7	9.9	5.7	-2.2	-1.6
Government consumption	4.6	2.4	3.3	4.5	3.7	1.2
Gross fixed capital formation	5.8	10.9	-14.0	23.9	-7.9	7.0
Of which:						
Residential construction	0.8	-1.4	4.2	11.5	-0.3	-4.4
Oil sector	112.6	49.8	-44.2	81.2	-18.0	-0.4
Ships and pipelines	-42.0	-51.8	-201.8	73.8	-97.9	–
Other business sector	-1.0	11.5	10.0	15.0	-18.7	-4.4
Government (excluding public enterprises)	5.2	2.4	-3.6	17.0	7.7	5.9
Final domestic demand	3.3	4.9	1.8	9.8	-2.6	1.3
Stockbuilding[1]	-1.8	1.0	2.7	-1.3	-0.8	-2.0
Total domestic demand	1.3	6.0	4.7	8.1	-3.4	-0.7
Exports of goods and services	7.6	8.2	6.9	1.9	2.0	3.1
Imports of goods and services	0.0	9.5	5.9	10.4	-6.8	-3.2
Foreign balance[1]	3.4	0.3	1.0	-3.1	3.7	2.4
GDP	4.6	5.7	5.3	4.2	0.5	1.7
Memorandum items:						
Mainland GDP	2.6	3.8	5.9	4.0	0.0	0.6
Mainland total domestic demand	-0.2	6.7	7.6	9.3	-1.8	-1.0
OECD Europe GDP	1.6	2.6	2.6	2.7	2.7	3.5

1. Contribution to GDP.
2. First three quarters of 1988 over first three quarters of 1987, 1986 prices.

Sources: Central Bureau of Statistics and OECD.

housing demand to higher debt servicing costs and subdued income growth has been slower. The downturn in Mainland *business investment* has been more pronounced, as it followed upon an even stronger rise in the mid-1980s than recorded for household demand. A high debt burden, falling profitability, and declining capacity utilisation – with the notable exception in some export industries – have put a damper on capital spending. The decrease has been particularly steep in manufacturing (disregarding oil refineries) but has also been quite sizeable in some service sectors. Offsetting developments in the offshore and public sectors are likely, however, to make for an increase in total fixed capital formation in 1988. *Oil investment* has weakened following a sharp increase in 1986; recorded investment has to be seen in connection with inventory changes (oil platforms being considered as fixed investment only at the time they are towed out to the field). Also, the transferral of ships to the new Norwegian International Ship Register is statistically recorded as shipping investment. *Public investment* has kept rising strongly at the central government level while municipalities appear to have adjusted capital spending to lower income growth, after two years of strong expansion.

The buoyancy of traditional exports in 1988 (for details, see below) seems to have just sufficed to arrest the fall in aggregate demand in 1988 as a whole. The weakness of demand components with a high import content, such as consumer durables and investment goods, led to a further decline in imports and allowed a modest rise in *real GDP*. The latter can be largely attributed to a marked expansion of oil output, notwithstanding continued production restraints in support of OPEC's attempt to stabilise oil prices. The virtual stagnation of Mainland GDP resulted from growing output in the primary and public sectors being offset by markedly declining output in the distribution sector with little change in construction and manufacturing production. Mirroring demand patterns, industries producing for the home market recorded some decline while some export-oriented industries, in particular non-ferrous metals producers, were able to increase output strongly and even faced capacity constraints. On the whole, however, there appears to have been no shift in the output structure towards the exposed sector: production continued to shrink in import-competing industries and stopped growing in sheltered industries only more recently.

Pronounced pick-up in unemployment

For more than a year after Mainland GDP had stopped rising in mid-1986 the labour market kept tightening: employment growth remained vigorous, the number of vacancies continued to grow and registered unemployed fell further (Diagram 6).

Diagram 6. **LABOUR MARKET DEVELOPMENTS**

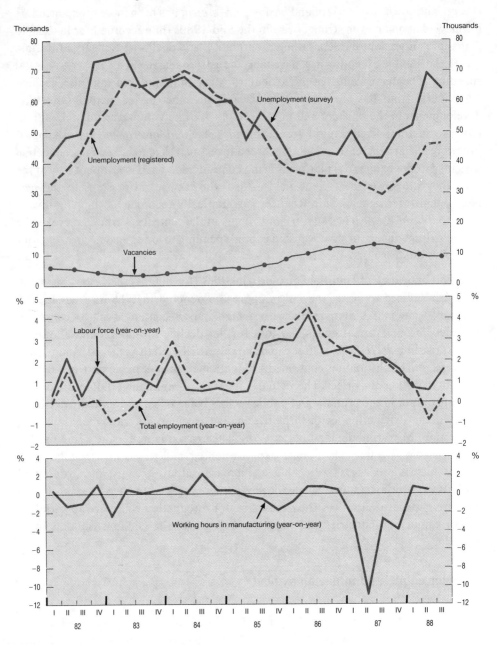

Sources: OECD, *Main Economic Indicators, Quarterly Labour Force Statistics.*

Only the widening gap between survey-based and registered unemployment data could be interpreted as indicating an incipient change in labour market conditions. Apart from the usual adjustment lags, the limited effect of weaker economic activity on employment can be mainly attributed to two factors: the reduction in standard working hours and an increase in public-sector employment. In 1987, high labour demand of both central and local governments more than outweighed reduced employment in some sectors of the economy, such as distribution and manufacturing. Despite an increase in overtime work and change-overs from part-time to full-time work, the shortening of the work-week reduced average working time by about 2 per cent in 1987. Yet, even on an hourly basis productivity performance deteriorated considerably, with the notable exception of manufacturing. Due to declines in some sectors, such as retail trade, hourly productivity appears to have virtually stagnated in the Mainland economy in 1987.

The situation changed markedly at the turn of 1987. With little change in output trends, labour demand started to decline: both the numbers of vacancies and of people in employment have dropped, entailing a general recovery in productivity growth. The petering out of the effects of the shortening of the work-week (Diagram 6) has contributed. But more important seems to have been the growing awareness that low activity growth was likely to persist and that employment levels had to be adjusted to falling profitability and domestic demand. Yet, there is little evidence of a shift of labour to the exposed non-oil sector of the economy. Within the industrial sector, reflecting productivity growth differentials, the downward adjustment of employment has been more pronounced in export-competing than in sheltered industries. The reduction in construction sector employment has been limited, and employment continued to grow, though at a slower pace, in private and public services other than distribution.

The downturn in employment has entailed a sharp rise in the number of unemployed, which doubled in the course of 1988 (Diagram 6). Registered unemployment has reached almost 3 per cent of the labour force, and survey data point to an even higher level. The number of job-seekers in manufacturing and construction has already surpassed the previous 1983/84 peak. The increase in unemployment has been damped by a marked drop in labour-force growth. In the three years before, labour supply had risen by almost 2 per cent per annum, more than twice the rate of growth of the population at working age. As a result, labour-force participation reached a very high level by international comparison, in particular for women, who had been attracted by buoyant demand for labour in the service sector. In 1988, this trend seems to have come to a halt. Youth unemployment, though still low, has risen more than average unemployment. Regional disparities have also increased: the labour market is persistently tight in the south-east with an unemployment rate below 1 per cent; but the top rate has moved from about 3 per cent to almost 5 per cent. Until mid-1988, the authorities had refrained from increasing employment measures, which had been progressively scaled down to about 1 per cent of the labour force. Since then, however, the Government has broadened the scope of existing schemes, and, as noted above, a further expansion is planned for 1989.

Progress on the inflation front

The decline in inflation, albeit hesitant at the beginning of 1988 and falling short of official objectives, has continued. The twelve-month increase in consumer prices is now approaching 6 per cent, a rate which was hoped to be reached by the end of 1987. The inflation differential between Norway and its trading partners, though narrowing, has remained substantial, and the temporary improvement in competitiveness stemming from the devaluation of the krone in 1986 has been eroded (Diagram 7). Still, conditions for disinflation have been favourable, with the rate of growth of both import prices and unit labour costs being halved in 1988 (Table 9). Imported inflation has receded, as the effects of the devaluation have petered out. In the course of 1988 the rise in labour costs has been curbed by the wage freeze currently in force (see below). Despite the depressed business situation, evidenced by the large number of firms reported to face grave financial problems and the steep increase in the number of liquidations, profit margins appear to have increased in the distribution sector as in the economy on average: the rise in the Mainland GDP deflator (around 7 per cent) is estimated to have outmatched the growth of unit labour costs by more than two percentage points. Estimates for 1988 are, however, still highly uncertain. Also, there is evidence that the profit situation differs widely, with very high earnings concentrated in a small number of industries, such as exporters of basic products.

With consumer price inflation running at around 7 per cent at the time of the spring 1988 wage round, the Government introduced legislation, aimed at limiting wage increases to less than 5 per cent on average in 1988. With wage carry-over at the beginning of 1988 in the LO/NAF area put at just below 3½ per cent, full compliance with the Income Regulation Act would result in wage increases of about 5 per cent in 1988. The year-on-year growth in hourly earnings in manufacturing of 7 per cent in the second quarter would seem to suggest that wagedrift has not completely disappeared. Notwithstanding a drop to about 5 per cent in the third quarter,

Diagram 7. **PRICES AND COSTS BY INTERNATIONAL COMPARISON**

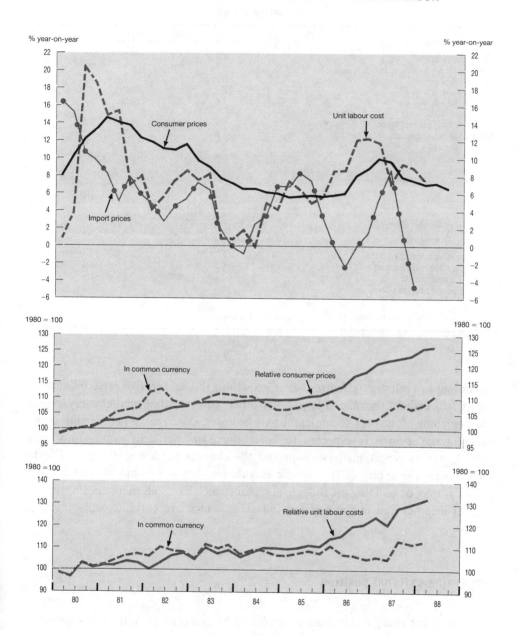

Sources: Central Bureau of Statistics; Bank of Norway; OECD estimates.

Table 9. **Prices, wages and incomes**
Percentage change

	1984	1985	1986	1987	1988[1]
Consumer prices	6.2	5.7	7.2	8.7	6½
Imported goods	5.7	5.9	9.9	9.3	5
Wholesale prices	6.2	5.0	2.4	6.2	5½
Raw materials	10.4	1.7	0.0	4.2	12
Fuel and energy	7.6	4.7	−10.5	6.7	2
Compensation per employee	6.9	7.5	9.0	8.3	6½
Hourly earnings, manufacturing	8.6	8.0	10.3	14.2	6
Unit labour costs	3.2	5.2	8.8	11.0	4½
Manufacturing	5.8	6.7	10.1	10.9	3
Disposable income of households					
Nominal	10.3	8.3	8.1	9.5	6
Real	3.7	2.3	0.6	1.3	0
National disposable income					
Nominal	14.6	12.5	1.8	7.8	5
Real	8.7	5.5	−5.1	−1.3	−1½
Growth contribution by:					
Net domestic product	6.3	6.4	4.8	0.4	0
Terms of trade	2.1	−2.0	−10.0	−1.9	−1
Interest and transfers, net	0.3	1.1	0.1	0.2	−½

1. Estimates.
Sources: Central Bureau of Statistics; Ministry of Finance; OECD estimates.

according to preliminary figures, wage growth in this sector, like price inflation, is likely to overshoot the official target. For other sectors with a smaller carry-over at the beginning of the year, the outcome may be lower, in particular in the public sector where wage growth is expected to be in the 3 to 4 per cent range. Less tight labour-market conditions have improved the chances for low settlements for the period after the expiry of the Income Regulation Act at the end of March 1989. Pressure may be building up, though, in sectors which have suffered a substantial fall in real incomes and in some export industries which are currently enjoying high profits.

Improving external position

Since the sharp swing from a surplus of 5½ per cent of GDP into a deficit of 6½ per cent in 1986, the current external balance has improved by about 2½ per cent in terms of GDP. The overall figures are distorted, however, by special factors, in particular the establishment of the Norwegian International Ship Register in 1987, which has reversed the previous trend towards registrations abroad and shows up in the current account as net imports of ships. Excluding this item, the current account deficit has more than halved since 1986. With some further decrease in the oil surplus, this favourable trend is attributable to the marked fall in the traditional trade deficit (Diagram 8). The latter overstates, however, the underlying improvement as it owes much to a cyclical boom in foreign trade in semi-manufactures. An assessment of the underlying trend in the external position also needs to take account of interest

Diagram 8. **CURRENT EXTERNAL ACCOUNT**
(Billion kroner)

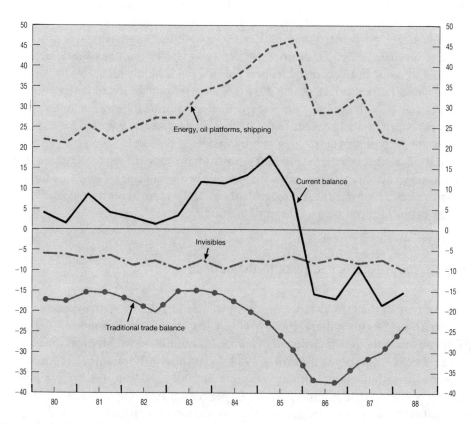

Source: Central Bureau of Statistics.

payments to foreigners resulting from the high net foreign debt of just under 20 per cent of GDP. The improvement in Norway's external position is perhaps best illustrated by the fall in the Mainland current account deficit (about 6 percentage points of Mainland GDP since 1986) back to the 1984 level.

The substantial strengthening in the traditional trade balance (merchandise trade, excluding oil, gas and ships) reflects both volume and price developments. The sizeable negative growth differential of domestic demand between Norway and its trading partners since mid-1986 has been the main factor behind diverging trends of import and export demand. The commodity composition of Norway's foreign trade has amplified this volume effect while at the same time making for a substantial improvement in the terms of trade. The rise in traditional *export* volumes in 1988 is likely to have surpassed the growth rate of 7½ per cent achieved a year earlier. Exports appear to have expanded broadly in line with geographical markets, despite an estimated loss in competitiveness of some 4 per cent since 1986. Norwegian exporters seem to have benefited from the commodity composition of world demand, which has been particularly buoyant for some traditional export products, such as non-ferrous metals. Basic industries are capital-intensive and thus less affected by high labour costs. In any case, their operation was made highly profitable by the steep rise in world market prices, which has significantly contributed to better (non-oil) terms of trade. With declining domestic demand, traditional *import* volumes appear to have dropped by about 6½ per cent for the second consecutive year in 1988, largely on account of continued destocking, tumbling sales of consumer durables and sharply reduced investment activity. Import substitution may have been fostered by diminishing capacity utilisation in import-competing industries and the surge in import prices following the 1986 devaluation. Only more recently has the rise in import prices dropped below that of domestic prices.

Short-term prospects and risks to the outlook

Activity in the OECD area has grown significantly faster than expected in the aftermath of the stock-market crisis. Given the strong cyclical momentum, real GDP growth in the area is projected to remain buoyant in the near term, falling below the 3 per cent mark only at the turn of 1989. Accordingly, the expansion of Norway's markets for manufactures, although expected to fall back from the current rate of about 9 per cent, could still run at about 7½ per cent in 1990. On the basis of constant nominal exchange rates, no change in Norway's competitive position is projected over the next two years. Nevertheless, given lagged effects of the previous deterioration and possible capacity constraints, exports of manufactures (excluding ships) are likely to grow less than markets. Strongly rising oil exports will, however, boost the overall result, even if, as assumed, the limitations on oil output (see above) remain in force. As discussed in Part II, the 1989 Budget implies no change in the fiscal stance and the same is assumed for 1990. Monetary policy is primarily aimed at securing capital inflows to support the exchange rate. This requires a high level of interest rates by international comparison. The projected fall in inflation and inflation differentials should, however, provide some scope for a decrease in nominal interest rates.

On these assumptions, the decline in domestic demand can be expected to continue in the near term but to come to a halt in the course of 1990 (Table 10). With modest growth in real disposable income of households, private consumption is likely

Table 10. **Short-term prospects**

Per cent volume change from previous year

	1988	1989	1990	Official forecast 1989[1]
Private consumption	-2½	-½	0	0.0
Public consumption	¾	1	2	1.2
Gross fixed investment	4½	-5¼	0	-6.4
Of which:				
Oil sector	11	6½	10	7.8
Housing sector	-1½	-2	-½	-1.0
Public sector	2¼	-7½	-1	-11.4
Other business sector	-8	-13	-4	-10.5
Final domestic demand	0	-1½	½	-1.6
Change in stocks[2]	-1½	-1	-½	-0.1
Total domestic demand	-1	-2¾	-¼	-1.7
Exports of goods and services	4	9¾	5¾	7.7
Imports of goods and services	-1½	-1	1	-1.9
Foreign balance[2]	1¾	5	2½	3.6
GDP	1	2½	2½	1.9
GDP deflator	5¼	½	2½	2.7
Private consumption deflator	5¾	4½	4	4.0
Employment	-¾	-½	¼	-0.8
Unemployment rate[3]	3	3½	3½	..
Memorandum items:				
Mainland GDP	-¼	-½	¼	-0.4
Total domestic demand, excluding investment in shipping and oil production	-2½	-2	0	-1.1

1. Fiscal Budget 1989, 1987 prices.
2. Contribution to GDP growth.
3. Level.

Sources: OECD and Ministry of Finance.

to be virtually flat through the next two years. Though turning positive, the household saving ratio is expected to remain low, as the scope for further spending cuts seems limited after the sharp fall in purchases of durables since 1986. Public consumption is projected to expand moderately in volume terms, and public investment to drop markedly; much will depend, though, on whether local authorities cut spending in response to lower revenue growth and high indebtedness, as assumed. Housing and commercial building starts point to continued weakness in construction activity. The substantial increase in lending quotas allotted to the State Housing Bank should, however, serve to support demand, even allowing for the accompanying reduction in interest rate subsidies. With depressed activity and uncertain growth expectations, the decline in Mainland business investment may continue. The current high level of profitability and capacity utilisation in some export industries may stimulate investment in that sector and partly compensate for lower capital spending by import-competing and service industries. The time profile of business investment will be influenced by the completion of a large oil refinery in 1989. Continued destocking reflects in part the adjustment of inventories to lower demand but also the acceleration in oil investment, as platforms under construction are statistically recorded as inventory investment.

The decline in domestic demand is projected to be outweighed by improvements in the real foreign balance which will be strengthened by international growth differentials and increased oil production. Real GDP may grow at a rate of 2½ per cent in both 1989 and 1990, while Mainland GDP could fall somewhat in 1989 before resuming growth in 1990. Mirroring output trends, the contraction of employment is likely to continue over most of the projection period. Labour-force participation rates are assumed to remain broadly stable. Even so, the unemployment rate may rise further before stabilising at about 3½ per cent. Less tight labour market conditions should entail a further reduction in wage increases, bringing unit labour cost developments in manufacturing into line with those of trading partners. Combined with projected moderate increases in import prices and some squeeze on profit margins, it should also help sustain the disinflation process.

The favourable effects of developments in the real foreign balance on the current external account are likely to be partly offset by worsening terms of trade (Table 11), largely attributable to offshore activities. On the assumption of constant oil prices in real terms, energy export prices will still be considerably below their 1988 level by 1990, given the sharp decline during the course of the past twelve months. The rapid expansion of oil output will nevertheless lead to a renewed rise in the surplus on oil trade. The adverse effects on the external account of the establishment of the Norwegian International Ship Register are likely to peter out. With little change in

Table 11. **Current external account projections**

	1988		1989		1990	
	Volume	Price	Volume	Price	Volume	Price
	Per cent changes from previous year					
Exports of goods	4¼	–1½	12¼	–4¾	6¾	1¼
Of which:						
Oil and gas[1]	8	–15	18¾	–12	8	–1
Traditional goods	9	8	5	3½	5	3½
Imports of goods	–3	2¼	–2½	3¼	½	3¼
Of which:						
Traditional goods	–6½	2½	¼	3¼	½	3½
	Norwegian kroner, million					
Trade balance	–1 484		7 651		14 443	
Invisibles, net	–20 621		–22 425		–22 699	
Current balance	–22 105		–14 774		–8 256	
Memorandum items:						
Current balance excluding						
ships and oil rigs	–14 920		–11 134		–4 615	
Mainland current balance	–65 493		–62 319		–59 342	

1. Based on a real oil price of U.S.$12.00 per barrel, and an exchange rate of Kr. 6.63 per U.S. dollar in 1989-90.
Source: OECD estimates.

the terms of trade for traditional goods, the improvement in the Mainland trade balance is projected to continue, though at a slower pace. Altogether, this is expected to result in a swing into surplus of the overall trade balance. The rising trend in the invisibles deficit, due mainly to growing foreign debt servicing, will damp, however, the improvement in the external balance. By 1990, the current account deficit may have narrowed to about 1½ per cent of GDP. (On the government oil-price assumption of about Kr. 90 or $14 per barrel, the deficit would be lower by about ¾ per cent of GDP.)

Downward risks to the outlook stemming from external developments would appear to be rather remote. In view of the recent buoyancy of activity in many Member countries, the economic expansion in the OECD area, and hence the growth of Norway's export markets, could be even stronger than projected in the near future. In these circumstances, a stronger rebound of oil prices than projected seems possible, though a renewed fall cannot be excluded either. On the domestic side, in the light of some recent indicators, activity may turn out to be weaker in the near term than projected. There are, however, also some features which could put at risk a continued reduction in external and internal imbalances. Public spending growth has accelerated, and there may be overruns, especially at the local level. Despite reduced pressures overall, there is still excessive demand in some segments of the labour market. Hence, there is an upward risk attached to the wage and price projections. As noted, wage pressures may be building up in sectors disadvantaged by the income freeze and some highly profitable export industries. High pay increases for some groups after the expiry of the Income Regulation Act could spread to other sections of the labour market thereby frustrating the Government's objective of closing the inflation gap in relation to trading partner countries. Much will depend on the responsiveness of wage-bargaining institutions to the economic adjustment needs and on the effectiveness of incomes policies, the historical record of which is examined in Part IV of this Survey.

IV. The labour market and wage formation

Progress made so far in correcting the external imbalance has essentially been achieved through domestic demand restraint, with consequential income and employment losses. A major rebalancing task therefore remains, if the economy is to return to an external surplus, while maintaining high employment levels. As noted in Part I, given the size of the outstanding adjustment problem, a considerable improvement in international competitiveness is necessary, while at the same time the exposed sectors must be able to attract resources from the sheltered sectors. The extent to which this can be achieved without a prolonged period of domestic demand restraint and rising labour market slack crucially depends on the behaviour of wage-setting institutions.

Labour market developments

A salient feature of the Norwegian labour market over the whole post-World War II era has been an exceptionally low level of unemployment. Indeed, at 1.6 per cent, the average unemployment rate in the 1960-86 period was the lowest recorded in any OECD country, except for Switzerland (Table 12). Parallel to most Member countries, unemployment rates drifted up after 1974, but much less than generally elsewhere. This outstanding record of low and broadly stable unemployment was achieved in spite of strong growth in the labour force, which outpaced that of the population of working age by an appreciable margin. The labour force participation rate, which had trailed the OECD average in the 1960s, had become one of the highest in the world by the mid-1980s.

Compared to other Member countries, the structure of unemployment displays both positive and negative aspects. On the positive side is the exceptionally small proportion of long-term unemployed (Table 13). Although nearly trebling in the course of the 1980s, its share in total unemployment remains the smallest in the

Table 12. **Labour market indicators**

	Unemployment rate		Labour force growth		Participation rate	
	1960-73	1973-86	1960-73	1973-86	1965	1985
Norway	**1.0**	**2.1**	**1.1**	**1.8**	**63.5**	**77.4**
United States	5.0	7.1	1.9	2.1	66.2	74.1
Japan	1.3	2.2	1.3	0.9	71.9	72.4
Germany	0.8	5.0	0.2	0.2	70.5	65.1
Sweden	1.6	2.4	0.6	0.8	72.9	81.0
Denmark	1.6	7.0	1.2	1.1	73.0	81.0
Austria	2.0	2.4	-0.2	0.4	70.3	65.8
Switzerland	..	0.5	1.3	0.0	79.0	71.4
OECD Europe	2.8	7.3	0.4	0.8	68.4	65.2

Source: OECD, *Labour Force Statistics*, various issues.

OECD area. A negative feature of the unemployment structure is the uneven incidence of joblessness across age groups and gender. The economy has not been as successful in keeping youth unemployment at bay as it has been in containing unemployment in general. About half of the people out of work are aged 16 to 24, a relatively high proportion for a mature industrialised country. Although youth unemployment rates compare favourably with most Member countries (Table 14), the differential between youth and total unemployment rates is high even though it has fallen since the last cyclical peak in 1980. The female unemployment rate has also persistently exceeded the total unemployment rate, though by a much smaller margin than that for youths. This is in line with the experience of other Northern European countries.

Table 13. **The structure of unemployment**
Per cent of total unemployment

	1980	1986	1980	1986	1979	1986
	Long-term unemployment[1]		Youth unemployment[2]		Female unemployment	
Norway	2.3	6.7	51.5	47.5	50.0	57.0
United States	4.3	8.7	45.8	37.7	49.0	45.0
Japan	16.0	17.2	21.1	23.5	36.8	40.1
Germany	17.0	32.0	27.3	24.6	52.4	46.1
Sweden	6.8	8.0	42.1	33.0	50.0	47.0

1. The term "long-term unemployment" refers to people out of work for twelve months and more.
2. The term "youth" refers to the 16 to 24 age group, except for Japan and Germany where it covers the 15 to 24 age group.
Source: OECD, *Employment Outlook*, September 1988, Paris 1988.

Table 14. **Incidence of unemployment**

	1980	1986	1980	1986	1979	1986
	Aggregate unemployment rate		Youth unemployment rate		Female unemployment rate	
Norway	1.7	2.0	5.4	5.4	2.4	2.6
United States	7.2	7.0	13.3	12.7	6.8	7.0
Japan	2.0	2.8	..	5.2	2.0	2.8
Germany	3.3	8.0	3.9	8.2	4.5	9.4
Sweden	1.6	2.2	5.1	5.6	2.3	2.7

Source: OECD, *Employment Outlook*, September 1987 and 1988, Paris, 1987 and 1988.

Official unemployment data may significantly understate the number of people who could be called into active employment, should labour demand increase. In Norway there are two main components of such "hidden labour reserves" (Table 15). One represents the so-called "discouraged workers", the other covers workers under special government labour schemes. "Discouraged workers" is a term used for people who want a job but are not actively seeking work. The reason for not engaging in active job search may be personal or some sense of frustration given the state of the labour market. According to survey evidence, the number of discouraged workers is very high relative to the number of unemployed persons. In 1979, discouraged workers actually exceeded total unemployment, and in the 1980s the ratio between the two groups never fell below 0.7. Although differences in survey methods and definitions make international comparisons difficult, this ratio seems surprisingly

Table 15. **Hidden labour reserves**
Per cent of total recorded unemployment

Year	Discouraged workers	Special labour market schemes	
		Total	Excluding rehabilitation
1979	126.3		
1980		46.5	23.0
1981		42.3	20.9
1982	78.9	33.1	18.6
1983	71.6	41.5	27.5
1984	73.8	55.6	38.0
1985	70.6	70.5	50.0
1986	90.0	59.6	32.3

Sources: OECD, *Employment Outlook*, September 1987, Paris 1987; OECD, *Labour Force Statistics 1965-1985*, Paris 1987; Statistisk Sentralbyra, *Arbeidsmarkedstatistikk 1986*, Oslo 1987.

high, in particular in the light of high participation rates. Of the countries where data on discouraged workers is available, Norway's ratio is exceeded only by that of Japan[1]. The other component of hidden labour reserves relates to special government labour market schemes providing employment for disabled people and other groups in need of rehabilitation and retraining. These schemes were expanded in the first half of the 1980s, when the number of people covered peaked (in 1985) at 70 per cent of the unemployed. Counting discouraged workers and people on labour market schemes as unemployed would certainly overstate the slack in the labour market, but allowing for their relative weight would reduce the wide "unemployment gap" between Norway and most other Member countries quite significantly.

The vigorous growth in employment, averaging 1½ per cent per annum between 1980 and 1988, was shared unevenly between the various sectors of the economy (Table 16). The growth of the oil sector required relatively little manpower: in the mid-1980s it absorbed only about 0.7 per cent of all jobs in the economy despite a contribution to GDP of about 18 per cent. However, obtaining about half of its investment goods from the Mainland, the oil sector has lent strong support to employment in the metal, machinery and equipment industries, without reversing the secular decline of manufacturing employment. As can be seen from Table 16, the share of employed in the primary and the secondary sectors has actually declined since the 1960s. Rapid growth of the tertiary sector meant that it was in a position to absorb workers released from the goods-producing sectors and the net increase in the labour force. Both private and, in particular, public sector employment expanded rapidly. In the mid-1980s, about a quarter of the total labour force was employed in the public sector, compared to some 20 per cent a decade earlier, a bigger increase than in most other Member countries.

Another notable feature of job creation since the mid-1970s has been the rapid growth of part-time employment paralleling stagnation of the full-time workforce. In

Table 16. **Sectoral employment shares**
Per cent

	1965	1975	1987
Primary sector	17.5	9.3	6.5
Secondary sector	36.4	34.3	26.5
Tertiary sector	46.1	56.4	66.9
Of which:			
General government	13.8	19.3	27.3

Sources: OECD, *Labour Force Statistics*, various issues.

1986, the number of part-time jobs was almost 50 per cent higher than in 1975, and more than a quarter of all the employed were working part time. As far as can be gauged from available data, part-time employment is of greater importance than in other Member countries[2]. This is true for both men and women. The buoyancy of part-time work means that participation rates overstate the extent to which labour supply has increased. Adjusting for part-time employment, the number of full-year equivalent workers as a proportion of the population at working age is roughly in line with major OECD countries (United States, Japan and Germany) and somewhat lower than in the other Nordic countries[3].

As regions have specialised in activities of their comparative advantage, structural changes inevitably impinge on regional employment patterns. The long-term trend has been for a movement of jobs from the northern to southern regions, and from rural to urban areas. These secular developments were interrupted in the 1970s, when important measures were taken to halt the trend. Regional mobility has prevented the emergence of substantial unemployment pockets. In fact, the dispersion of regional unemployment rates has narrowed since the 1970s. However, there remains a clear pattern of differing labour market pressures along regional lines, with above-average unemployment rates persistently recorded in the same districts.

Wage increases and industry wage structure

Despite much lower unemployment, Norwegian wages have advanced for a long time at similar rates on average to those in other Member countries (Diagram 9). This may, to an important extent, be credited to existing labour market institutions. In the 1970s, with wages developing broadly parallel with those in trading partner countries (Diagram 10), the deterioration in cost competitiveness was exclusively due to an appreciation of the currency and relatively slow labour productivity growth. The situation changed, however, in the 1980s when the OECD area went through a process of sharp wage disinflation. Though some deceleration in wage growth also occurred in Norway, it fell far short of matching disinflation abroad. In the 1980-87 period, the wage increase in Norway was more than a quarter higher than in trading partner countries. Devaluation of the krone in 1986 and somewhat better productivity developments were not sufficient to outweigh the relative increase in wages. Hence, between 1980 and 1987 Norway's international competitiveness, as measured by unit labour costs in common currency, deteriorated by 12 per cent. Judged against labour market pressures in the 1980s, wage developments may still be labelled moderate;

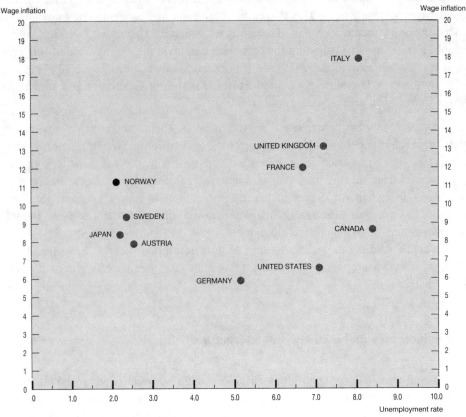

Diagram 9. **WAGE INCREASES AND UNEMPLOYMENT**
(1973-1987 averages)

Sources: OECD, *Main Economic Indicators, Labour Force Statistics.*

however, compared to developments abroad, wage increases have significantly exceeded the rate compatible with maintaining a healthy external balance. With oil revenues no longer cushioning the external position from declining competitiveness, the challenge to labour market institutions is to correct misalignments in costs without a sharp rise in unemployment.

While differential wage cost growth has an important bearing on a country's ability to compete internationally, the wage structure plays a prominent role in the allocation of labour. The evolution of wages since 1970 shows that, in general, pay increases for low income groups have exceeded those for high income groups and wage differentials have been compressed across different industries, gender and educational backgrounds (Diagram 11). The wage ratio between industrial sectors registering the highest and lowest wage was 1.57 in 1970; by 1987 this figure had fallen to 1.36. The ranking relative to the average wage of blue-collar workers in manufacturing changed somewhat during this period. The most notable changes were the regression of public sector wages compared with private sector wages and some gains in some fast-growing private services. The wage gap for female against

Diagram 10. **INTERNATIONAL COMPETITIVENESS IN MANUFACTURING**

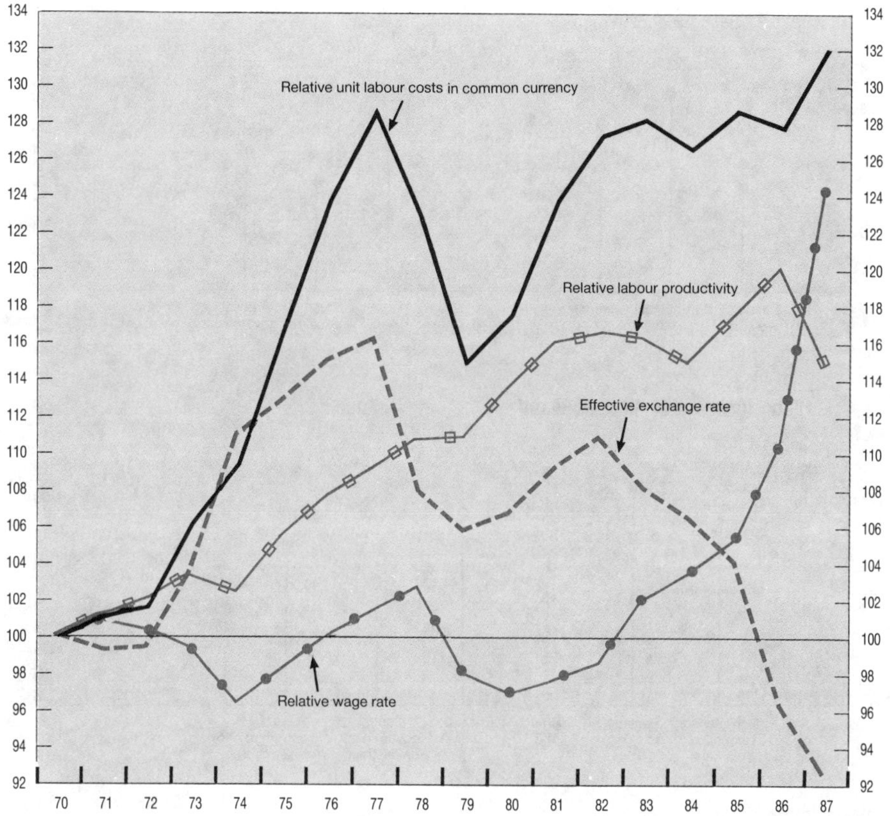

Source: OECD estimates.

Diagram 11. **OCCUPATIONAL WAGE STRUCTURE**

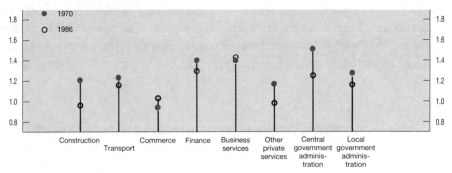

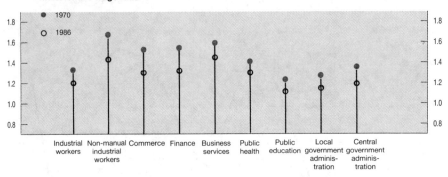

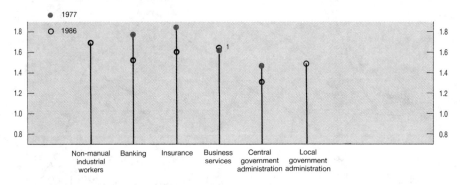

1. 1980 and 1986 figures.
2. Higher education refers to university and technical education.

Source: Norges Offentlige Utredninger, *Inntektsdannelsen i Norge,* (NOU 1988: 24), Oslo 1988.

male workers also narrowed somewhat in the 1970-1985 period. The size of this gap has varied considerably from one sector to another. In the early 1970s, the male/female wage ratio was in the range of 1.25 to 1.67, narrowing to 1.14 to 1.45 by the mid-1980s. Wage differentials have been more pronounced between various educational backgrounds than between either occupational sectors or gender. This is particularly evident for the private sector where salaries of university graduates still exceed those of workers in manufacturing by about 50 per cent after having experienced a sharp relative fall in the 1970s.

Norwegian wages appear to be more even than in many Member countries, but international comparisons in this area must be treated with caution given differences in definitions. With non-manual yearly wages exceeding manual yearly wages by one-third, the differential in Norway seems only somewhat larger than in Japan but lower than in the other major OECD countries, notably compared with the United States, France and Germany[4]. The male/female earnings ratio is lower than in any country for which data are available, except Sweden[5].

Institutions of wage determination

Institutional labour-market arrangements may have important bearings on the success of countries in coping with sustained pressures on human resources and in adapting to structural changes in labour demand and supply conditions. A dominant characteristic of the Norwegian collective bargaining system is the high degree of centralisation. Another prominent feature is the relatively active part which the Government plays in influencing labour market outcomes. For decades, incomes policy has played a major role in overall economic policymaking. To facilitate the implementation of such policies, a number of institutions have been created, serving to strengthen the centralisation of wage determination.

Unions and employers' federations

Trade-union membership has been relatively stable over the last two decades, with some edging up in the 1980s. At close to 60 per cent of the total dependent labour force, the overall unionisation rate, though lower than in the other Nordic countries, by far exceeds that of most other Member countries (Table 17). The degree of unionisation varies markedly between different sectors of the economy (Table 18). The public sector has the highest proportion of employees organised in unions, followed by the financial sector, manufacturing, and transport. Other private services sectors, such as wholesale and retail trade, have comparatively low union membership.

Table 17. **Trade union membership as a percentage of total labour force**

Norway (1983)	56
United States (1984)	15
Japan (1982)	22
Germany (1981)	35
Sweden (1984)	79
Denmark (1984)	73
Finland (1984)	68

Source: OECD, *Structural Adjustment and Economic Performance*, Paris 1987.

Table 18. **Trade union membership by sector and affiliation**

	Per cent organised in 1985 by:				
	LO	YS	AF	Others	Total
Primary sectors	11	2	–	–	13
Petroleum and gas production	42	–	–	26	68
Manufacturing and mining	61	3	4	3	71
Construction and power supply	52	1	3	–	56
Commerce	22	2	–	3	27
Sea transport	39	–	–	32	71
Other transport	61	11	1	1	74
Financial services	5	61	9	5	80
Other private services	17	1	7	1	27
Public sector	31	11	15	24	81

Note: LO: Norwegian Federation of Trade Unions
YS: Confederation of Vocational Unions
AF: Federation of Norwegian Professional Associations
Source: Norges Offentlige Utredninger, *Inntektsdannelsen i Norge*, (NOU 1988: 24), Oslo 1988.

In 1985, unionised workers were organised into 168 separate unions. Most of these are affiliated to one of the three major union confederations. The largest of these is the Norwegian Federation of Trade Unions, *Landsorganisasjonen i Norge* (LO), with 36 affiliated unions. In the early 1970s, this was the only major trade union federation, but in the course of the 1970s other coalitions emerged: the Confederation of Vocational Unions, *Yrkesorganisasjonens Sentralforbund* (YS), and the Federation of Norwegian Professional Association, *Akademikernes Fellesorganisasjon* (AF). These two organisations covered 72 and 36 unions, respectively in

1985. The new federations were primarily formed by unions which had not been affiliated to the LO. Consequently, their creation did not result in a sharp decline of LO membership. However, the proportion of unionised workers belonging to the LO has gradually declined over the past twenty years or so. In 1970, it covered nearly three-quarters of all unionised workers; by 1985 the proportion had fallen to 60 per cent. This decline reflects both competition between rival federations and structural employment changes. The competition for members is most intense in the public sector, where the LO covers the great majority of unskilled workers. The traditional domain of the LO has, however, been manufacturing which has experienced an absolute drop in employment due to declining international competitiveness. As the LO covers the majority of workers in the exposed sectors it must play a crucial role in the necessary process of rebalancing the economy in coming years.

On the employers' side, there are two major federations, one catering for the private sector, the other for the public sector. The Norwegian Employers' Confederation, *Norsk Arbeidsgiverforening* (NAF), organises employers in manufacturing, oil and mining activity, construction and some services. Establishments affiliated to NAF employed about somewhat less than a fifth of the total workforce in 1986, but the share has declined over the last decades in parallel to the shrinking manufacturing activity. These structural changes have increased the importance of employers' associations outside NAF, especially in commerce and financial services. In 1986, private employers' confederations outside the NAF area employed about 9 per cent of all wage earners. Employment trends have increased the importance of the public sector as an employer. There are two bargaining units: the central government and the Confederation of Municipalities, but bargaining is co-ordinated between the two. Together they cover more employees than the NAF.

Although the number of people covered by agreements between LO and NAF has fallen rapidly since the 1960s, LO/NAF settlements still play a key role as pace-setters in bargaining rounds. Once a LO/NAF settlement has been struck bargaining starts in the public sector, with outcomes strongly influenced by LO/NAF agreements. Over the last two decades there has only been one exception to this pattern. The timing of bargaining in other sectors, notably banking, is less regular. Settlements reached between the LO and NAF are also extended to non-union workers in all establishments affiliated to the NAF. Moreover, LO/NAF agreements are frequently taken over by non-member firms where the workers may or may not be unionised. The traditional pace-setting role of LO/NAF agreements has for a long time made the exposed sector the wage leader in the economy. The growing proportion of workers in the LO/NAF sphere of influence whose jobs are not directly threatened by foreign competition may, however, have made these organisations more inward-looking than before. The fact that LO/NAF settlements also cover the petroleum industry and oil-related sectors, may also have influenced bargaining behaviour.

Central and local wage agreements – wagedrift

Despite the centralised wage-bargaining system, a considerable part of wage increases tends to be determined outside bargaining between unions and employers' federations. Occasionally, there were even no wage settlements at the national level in the LO/NAF area. Such "unco-ordinated" bargaining took place in 1981-82 and 1985-86. For many employees, wage contracts can be concluded on three or four different levels: nationwide bargaining, industry-wide bargaining, enterprise bargaining and bargaining between individual employees and employers. Wagedrift – the difference between actual wage increases and increases negotiated at the central level – varies significantly from industry to industry. Since the 1960s, wagedrift in manufacturing has on average accounted for more than half of total annual wage increases, and over the last decade it has contributed more than three-quarters (Diagram 12). Wagedrift is largely absent in the public sector. Its growing relative importance in the private sector reflects moderation in centrally-negotiated tariff growth rather than rising wagedrift in itself.

The historical background for local bargaining in the LO/NAF area is that centrally-negotiated wage contracts were used to set minimum wages. Firms were expected to increase payments beyond the contractual minimum, originally through piece rates which forged a link between enterprise labour costs and efficiency. Since the mid-1960s, the role of piece rates has declined significantly, but the locally-negotiated supplement has been retained in contract areas with minimum wage agreements. Local bargaining has been introduced in more and more sectors since the 1960s, making all central wage agreements in the LO/NAF area in fact minimum contracts.

Union and employers' federations have limited authority over local bargaining, and outcomes often exceed initial expectations. Industry-wide bargaining is not completely unco-ordinated as LO and NAF are usually acting behind the scenes. The central organisations have also agreed not to use strikes and lockouts in local bargaining. The few local strikes which took place at this level were thus illegal. However, workers may threaten to withdraw co-operation in various ways, leading to formal or informal "go-slow" and "work-to-rule" actions. In the metal industry, for example, "go slow" actions have become more or less institutionalised as a legal

Diagram 12. **CENTRALLY-DETERMINED WAGES AND WAGE DRIFT**
(First quarter to first quarter)

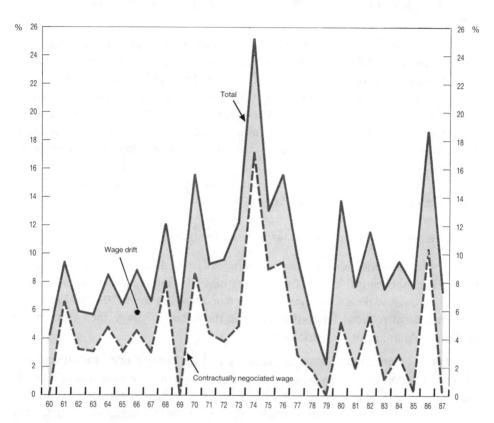

Source: N.A.F.'s wage statistics.

conflict weapon. At the enterprise level, the power of the central federations is reduced to moral suasion.

Wage contracts: duration and scope

Since the mid-1960s, the contract period of central wage settlements has without exception been two years. Agreements have always had some provision for inflation adjustment after the first year. Earlier there were indexation clauses, which gave partial compensation if the consumer price index passed a predetermined level. Since the 1960s, it has been more common for intermediate bargaining rounds to take place on fixed dates. This has also allowed the bargaining parties to bring in other issues for review.

Central wage contracts rarely reduce management prerogatives but they typically embody solidaristic goals of the union movement. Since the 1960s, no major central agreement has been concluded in the LO/NAF area without special provisions for low-wage workers. Wage compression benefited enterprises with a relatively highly paid work-force. Attempting to even out the effects of wage compression on firms' profits, a special fund was established in 1980, which received contributions from all establishments and distributed them to low-wage firms. In the first half of the 1980s when unemployment was relatively high, the low-wage premium was reduced in some sectors as it was thought to threaten employment for certain categories of unskilled workers.

Government involvement in wage settlements

Norwegian governments have traditionally tried to influence bargaining outcomes at the central level. At times they have also intervened in the bargaining process through various legal means. On two occasions in the 1970s and 1980s, the Government introduced legislation to limit the extent of wage increases and to contain the damage of industrial strife.

The laws governing industrial disputes call for compulsory arbitration for a prolonged period before any nationwide strike or lock-out can take place. This has undoubtedly contributed to the low strike frequency compared with other countries. The State Arbitrator, who is usually engaged in every bargaining round, may facilitate the reaching of agreements between the social partners. Parliament has several times passed special laws to prevent or stop strikes, referring the disputes to a special commission which can impose a solution. Disputes between LO and NAF were referred to this commission in 1978 and 1981 but it has been called upon more often to settle disputes in the public sector. The most drastic form of government intervention is to rule by decree, either freezing wages or limiting wage increases. Following a complete deadlock of negotiations in the autumn of 1978, the Government instituted a general wage freeze which remained in force until late 1979 and as noted earlier, the 1988 Income Regulation Act, which was enacted in support of the government's incomes policy, set a ceiling on permissible wage increases.

Since the early 1960s the Contact Committee has played a central role in incomes policy. It is headed by the Prime Minister and consists of senior Cabinet members, representatives of farmers and fishermen, and the leaders of the main employers and employees' federations. The purpose of the Committee is to exchange information, prior to bilateral negotiation, about income objectives and the economic outlook. Since the mid-1960s the economic situation and prospects for the pending bargaining period have been evaluated in detail by the Technical Reporting Committee on the Income Settlement (TRC). This Committee consists of economists from both the LO and NAF as well as economists from ministries and an official research institute. Its task is to give statistical background information, arrive at a common view about economic developments, and to discuss the implications of different bargaining outcomes on the economy. For this purpose the Committee uses the same macroeconomic model as the Government does in preparing its economic policy. Both the Contact Committee and the TRC have served the purpose of increasing information available to both sides of industry, and of narrowing down disagreements stemming from different perceptions about the future.

In practice, Norwegian incomes policy has gone beyond facilitating discussion among the social partners and offering technical assistance. The government has repeatedly offered a broad range of measures, such as increased public spending and tax benefits, in exchange for moderate wage settlements in the LO/NAF area. This approach reached its zenith in 1975, 1976 and 1977, when the Government was drawn directly into the bargaining process as a third party. In the face of growing income aspirations of unions, this form of tripartite bargaining was eventually seen to have yielded disappointing results. Between 1980 and 1987, the Government was not directly involved in wage bargaining. In more recent years, however, measures have been taken in line with proposals from the social partners (see Part II).

Wage formation

It is important to examine whether the growing gap between the level of wages in Norway and its main trading partners reflects an inherent deficiency in the wage-setting system, or whether the system has been put under too strong pressure. Determining the factors which influence wage inflation holds the key to the possible role of the labour market in improving international competitiveness and in stimulating resource flows to the exposed sector. These issues can best be assessed on the basis of available quantitative analyses. The traditional framework, relating changes in real wages in the long run to the level of unemployment, emphasises the role of market forces in changing wages. More recently, alternative models of wage determination have been proposed. Efficiency wage theories stress the heterogeneity of human resources and the role of the wage rate in stimulating work efficiency. A different framework is based on explicit models of bargaining between unions and employers' coalitions, using game theory to give insights into negotiation strategies and outcomes. Theories which emphasise the distinction between insiders and outsiders in the labour market, the role of work experience in human capital formation and turnover costs, have also been used to explain wage developments in some countries.

Annex I discusses these theories in greater detail. A common feature of the new models is that despite recognition given to labour-market conditions in explaining wage developments, the self-equilibrating market mechanism is more or less switched off. To the extent that these models represent the real world, this could have fundamental implications for economic policy-making. Discriminating between different model frameworks by reference to past experience is, however, extremely difficult and usually leads to inconclusive results. For example, studies suggest that Norwegian wage developments can be explained by either the traditional framework or the bargaining approach[6]. The OECD Secretariat's analytical work for most countries has been based on the traditional framework, as there is a presumption that market forces work in the labour market as in other markets, though often with longer lags.

The capacity to pay and consumer prices

As the remuneration for equal skills and labour qualifications cannot for long differ between domestically-oriented and internationally-competing sectors, the capacity of any economy to raise the average level of wages is closely linked to productivity trends in the exposed sector and the price of its products in world markets, expressed in domestic currency. No country can afford to have persistent misalignment between its unit labour costs and world market prices without compromising economic performance and running into balance-of-payments difficulties. The sooner wages adjust, the less disruption to employment. The capability to adjust income claims to supply shocks and changing demand conditions should be particularly strong in a bargaining system as highly developed as the Norwegian one.

The so-called Scandinavian model of inflation was indeed designed to highlight the role of external price trends and productivity developments on wage and income formation[7]. The model purported to explain wage developments but was also used by the TRC to assess the room for wage increases. Within this framework the different constraints facing exposed and sheltered industries can be highlighted and the implications for wage and price setting discussed. The exposed sector is postulated to set the pace in wage settlements with wages in the sheltered sector following suit, reflecting solidaristic wage policy or competition between sectors for (assumed) scarce labour. Wages in the exposed sector are expected to adjust over time to keep the distributional shares of labour and capital at some normal level. Product prices in the exposed sector are determined abroad and by the exchange rate, while prices in the sheltered sector adjust to keep profit shares constant. Taken together, these mechanisms would ensure that competitiveness remains unchanged over time, and immune from efficiency changes and alterations in the nominal exchange rate. However, the model has clearly failed to pass the test of time both as a forecasting device and an explanatory tool of past developments, the principal reason being that the forces which were thought to preserve international competitiveness of traditional industries were prevented from working.

The adjustment mechanisms on which the Scandinavian model relied failed to work once Norway emerged as a strong and growing oil exporter. The model presumed that should competitiveness deviate from the level which was consistent with normal distributional shares, a number of forces would come into play to correct the misalignment. Abnormally low profits would be taken as a sign by the trade unions to moderate wage claims and would increase the employers' resolve to resist excessive claims. Should unions nevertheless succeed in obtaining large wage increases, the ensuing loss in competitiveness would endanger jobs if domestic demand could not fill the gap left by foreign demand. Even then, the balance-of-payments implications of the deterioration in competitiveness would sooner or later prompt the Government to take deflationary measures and thus weaken the labour market still further.

In the event, the oil export revenues in the 1970s and up to the mid-1980s, and in particular prospects of large future gains, relieved the economy of balance-of-payments constraints. Spending of the oil money resulted in very buoyant domestic demand, thus minimising the disruption to jobs from the deterioration in competitiveness. The sectors which stood to lose most from the economy's inability to compete with foreign goods often also gained most from the growth in the oil sector. Moreover, accommodating exchange rate policy further undermined the self-equilibrating mechanism presumed to exist in the Scandinavian model. The situation changed dramatically after the oil price collapse. With the current balance of payments in large deficit and no immediate prospects of being "rescued" by oil as in the post-1979 period, there is clearly a need to revitalise and to broaden the exposed sector by re-establishing a close link between wage developments and the capacity to pay of existing and new internationally-competing industries.

Empirical analyses, built on the traditional wage inflation framework, continue to reveal effects from world prices and productivity on manufacturing wages, without supporting strict proportionality between these variables embedded in the Scandinavian model. Thus, a once-and-for-all change in the level of labour productivity or in the nominal exchange rate will have sustained effects on the level of competitiveness. The wage inflation response to a sustained increase in labour productivity advances varies markedly across different studies, and appears to be extremely sensitive to the accompanying explanatory variables. Recent studies suggest that there may be a unitary response between the two variables in the long-run, but that it takes time for the effects to work through. The wage inflation response from a permanent increase in external (import) prices is also very difficult to gauge with any precision, as it is closely correlated with the domestic price level. The long-run response is in the range 0.12 to 0.95, depending on the role given to other price variables.

While world prices influence the economy's ability to afford wage increases without negative consequences for the balance of payments, developments in consumer prices determine the extent to which a given wage increase may translate into extra real consumption. In order to ensure rising living standards, trade unions will pay close attention to consumption wages as reflected in indexation clauses. Over the last two decades, consumer-price inflation has generally exceeded growth of producer prices in manufacturing. This is indeed a natural outcome as long as manufacturing productivity increases faster than that in the rest of the economy. However, to the extent that price differentials exceed productivity differentials, tensions in collective bargaining are likely to occur, intensifying the income distribution struggle. Wage inflation studies in Norway give developments in consumer prices a relatively small role compared with external prices, but in practice it may be difficult to disentangle effects from consumer prices and external prices.

According to the studies discussed above, it would seem that the Government has a number of options to influence wages and competitiveness. One is to change the nominal exchange rate; this could result in a lasting change in competitiveness, even after allowing for all the feedback effects. This option is fraught with danger, however, as it may fuel inflationary expectations and thus create unrest on the foreign-exchange market. This danger is the greater, the closer the economy is to working at full capacity. A different strategy would be to seek to stimulate productivity growth via supply-side policies. There may be doubts as to what extent increased efficiency would improve competitiveness, since the link between wages and productivity growth may be too strong to allow an appreciable impact. In fact, Norwegian models suggest that had the exposed sector been able to achieve the productivity growth rates of trading partners in the 1972-87 period, the deterioration in competitiveness would still have been important. However, improving efficiency in the sheltered sectors might offer an indirect way to improve competitiveness through its favourable impact on consumer prices and hence on wages. Another way to put downward pressure on consumer prices would be to sharpen competition in the sheltered sector. A precondition for any disinflationary device to work is the absence of excessive labour market pressure. Indeed, the tightness of the labour market has meant that there was a bidding-up of wages in the sheltered sectors of the economy with consequent increases in consumer prices. The demonstration effect of fast-growing wages in sheltered industries together with rapidly rising consumer prices has reinforced cost pressure in the traditional export and import-competing sectors, weakening the non-oil foreign balance despite devaluations of the currency.

Unemployment

Studies on wage behaviour in Norway, based on the traditional market framework, generally find a link between labour market pressure and growth in wages. The strength of the effect varies considerably from one study to another and is dependent on the period under consideration as well as other explanatory variables. The sustainable unemployment rate, which would keep competitiveness constant for given growth rates of world market prices and productivity, differs accordingly between models. For reasonable values of the variable determining the economy's ability to pay, this "equilibrium rate" is found to be in the range of 2½ to 3 per cent. A salient feature of the studies is that the strength of the labour-market pressure on wage inflation varies strongly with the level of unemployment. At an unemployment rate well below the "equilibrium rate", the upward pressure on wages is very strong. As the economy approaches this rate the upward pressure on wages diminishes rapidly, and somewhat beyond this rate an increase in unemployment would no longer add much to disinflationary pressure. The Norwegian economy has, however, rarely operated at unemployment levels around and above the suggested sustainable rate. This implies that these models may become inappropriate should the economy experience unemployment rates in excess of past experience. As hysteresis effects cannot be excluded, the exact value of the "equilibrium rate" may also be subject to a considerable degree of uncertainty.

Judged by past experience, there is a presumption that the sustainable unemployment rate is substantially lower than in most Member countries. Various explanations have been offered for the disparities of equilibrium unemployment rates across industrialised countries: differences in work ethics, the stance of public policy, including social security protection, demographic factors and perhaps most important in the case of Norway, differences in the organisation of collective-bargaining institutions. Highly centralised and highly decentralised bargaining systems appear to have features which are conducive to reducing the inflationary impact associated with slack in the labour market[8]. Bargaining institutions which fall between these two opposites are frequently found in countries with poor inflation performance and high unemployment.

A number of factors seem to have contributed to the good labour-market performance in Norway. Firstly, centralised bargaining across industries may make unions more aware of the cost, in terms of lost employment, of insisting on excessive nominal wage increases. Second, centralised bargaining allows negotiations to be conducted simultaneously, thereby reducing the danger of leap-frogging. Indeed, it was with the view of containing wage-wage spiral effects that the authorities pressed the social partners to move towards simultaneous bargaining across industries. Third, centralised bargaining circumvents the dilemma for a single union of accepting wage moderation without certainty that other unions will follow suit. Finally, centralised federations may be better equipped to assess the economy's ability to accommodate wage increases without jeopardising external and internal financial balance. As discussed earlier, incomes-policy institutions have aimed at providing the LO and NAF with information about the state of the economy and the economic outlook. The dissemination of such information could also have a moderating influence at the local level. The existence of multi-tier bargaining levels weakens the argument that it is centralisation alone which deserves credit for the favourable outcome. Wagedrift may also have prevented fragmentation of centralised bargaining by allowing unions at the federal level to be relieved at the local level.

There is some evidence that apart from moderating wage inflation, an increase in unemployment was accompanied by shifts in relative wages between sectors. In the past, manufacturing wages have tended to fall relative to non-manufacturing wages. The observed fall in relative wages in manufacturing as a result of an increase in unemployment seems difficult to explain. If this was really the case, the desirable resource flow to the exposed sector would be hampered as its increased demand for labour would coincide with reduced incentives for workers to move into the exposed sector. However, the behaviour of relative wages during periods of high or rising unemployment must certainly be influenced by the origin of the labour market slack. If unemployment rises owing to difficulties in the exposed sector, which was typically the case in the past, then a fall in relative wages for manufacturing seems a natural consequence. The opposite should happen when unemployment increases are concentrated in the sheltered sector.

Institutional factors

Overall wage developments are likely to be affected by the extent to which wages are determined at the central or local level, as bargainers at the various levels may have different perceptions about warranted wage increases and the risks involved in the economic outlook. They may, moreover, disagree about distributional questions, such as compression clauses, and other matters bearing on the evolution of wages. As discussed above, the institutional organisation of the two sides of industry, as well as government involvement in the wage formation process and its relations to the social partners, could help to explain differences in wage and labour market performances across countries.

a) *Determinants of tariffs and wagedrift*

As noted above, centrally-agreed tariff (base wage) increases and wagedrift have exhibited a markedly different evolution since the 1970s, suggesting that these two wage components are driven by different forces. Wagedrift has remained relatively stable throughout the period, while centrally-negotiated wages show big fluctuations. A recent Norwegian study, confined to manufacturing, concluded that tariff increases were much more responsive to macroeconomic forces than was wagedrift. This, however, seems to be a special feature of the 1980s. Up to the late 1970s, there was little correlation between centrally-negotiated wages and macroeconomic fundamentals. The rise in unemployment in 1983-84 and the subsequent fall were mirrored at the central level in wage moderation, followed by more assertiveness. In contrast, wagedrift remained fairly stable. These developments are clearly at variance with previously established links between the state of the labour market and the two wage components. Perhaps not surprisingly, wagedrift appears to be closely correlated with world market prices but, contrary to the generally perceived rationale for local settlements, it is difficult to find any robust relationship between productivity developments and wagedrift.

b) *Solidaristic wage policy and wage inflation*

Evening-out disparities in personal incomes has been a long-standing goal of the trade union movement. Wage compression clauses in central wage agreements and incomes-policy measures with a "social profile" bear witness to this objective. Income distribution among wage earners narrowed somewhat in the 1970s, but this process has stalled in the 1980s. The reduction in income disparity appears to be principally due to wage compression in the public sector and a more egalitarian wage structure between males and females (see above). In the private sector actual wage compression would seem to have been less pronounced than might have been expected from the solidaristic wage policy pursued at the central level. It is a common feature across many countries, where trade unions actively pursue redistributive aims, that wage compression at the central level is partly undone at the local level.

The evidence about repercussions of wage compression in central wage agreements on wagedrift is inconclusive. On the one hand, there is a significant correlation between tariff increases in low-wage sectors and wagedrift in high-wage sectors. On the other hand, it is difficult to find an independent effect of tariff increases in low-wage sectors on wagedrift in high-wage sectors, once other economic arguments such as unemployment, external and domestic prices are introduced. Furthermore, it is questionable whether wagedrift adjusts to tariff increases or *vice versa*. Many low-income sectors traditionally receive most of their wage increase in the form of tariff increases, while wagedrift accounts for a greater proportion of total wage increases in high-income sectors. Tariff increases may thus simply restore differentials for low-wage sectors, which widen during the contract period as a result of wagedrift. What seems clear is that relative wages play an important role in the dynamics of wage evolution.

Narrowing of wage differentials may reflect growing homogeneity of the labour force and reduction in rental income elements. Institutionally-driven wage compression across different markets facing different supply and demand conditions may, however, seriously weaken the allocative role of the wage system. Firms may not be able to attract workers from other occupations, students may not be attracted to socially most productive occupations, and there may be a tendency for firms to overuse high-quality human resources if the cost to the firms is less than the cost to society of producing these resources. On the other hand, raising wages at the bottom end of the income scale will reduce the availability of low-productivity jobs and hence prompt low-wage earners to acquire higher skills or otherwise to intensify the search for more productive jobs. This is a particularly positive feature if labour resources are scarce.

It is arguable that wage compression in the private sector was not institutionally driven. Reduction in the male/female wage ratio may reflect the fact that women entering the labour market have higher educational qualifications than before. Also, the reduction in the education premium could have come about by increased supply of workers with higher education. Wage compression in the public sector, much more pronounced than in the private sector, could also be explained in a similar way.

However, it is also likely to mirror the powerful position of the public sector as the sole or principal employer of important professional groups, e.g. teachers and nurses. Some occupations may be able to have compensation for reduced relative wages, such as less intensive work. In this case, wage compression could entail efficiency losses. The long-run effects of falling differentials in occupations without any compensation may, however, show up in increasing difficulties for the Government in attracting qualified personnel.

c) *Wage inflation and direct government involvement*

There is some evidence that direct government involvement in the wage formation process has had a moderating influence on wages. In spite of adverse macroeconomic forces, the 1978/79 wage freeze succeeded in reducing wage inflation during the period covered by legislation. A sharp acceleration of wages marked the immediate post-freeze period, but the state of the economy at the time was such that it could have produced such an increase in any event. Thus, the freeze may have had lasting positive effects on international competitiveness. Care should be taken, however, not to generalise from a single event. When the provisions of the 1988 Income Regulation Act expire in spring 1989, economic conditions are likely to be much weaker than after the 1978/79 freeze. Should wage inflation nevertheless pick up, the claim that wage freezes have lasting effects on inflation and competitiveness would weaken.

As discussed earlier, incomes policy has occasionally included the granting of tax relief in exchange for wage moderation at the central level. The rationale for this policy was that workers would recognise tax cuts as having the same effects on their post-tax income as an increase in their pre-tax wage. However, once workers or their representatives react to tax changes, the net effects on wages become ambiguous. Reduction in marginal tax rates stimulates labour supply with beneficial effects on inflation, while a reduction in the average tax rate may pull in the other direction. The impact on union wage claims is also ambiguous as a reduction in marginal tax rates raises the cost in terms of forgone disposable income growth for keeping unemployment low, while the opposite is true if the average tax rate is cut. Against this background, it is not surprising that empirical studies have difficulties in finding well-determined relationships between tax rates and wages. However, the summary measures of the tax system employed in these studies, such as average or marginal tax rates for a specific household, may not capture the effects of tax changes. The ambiguous effects, on *a priori* reasoning, should caution policy-makers against the use of tax concessions in the pursuit of stabilisation policies. Reduction in marginal tax rates could, however, stimulate growth through its efficiency-enhancing effects and this might well improve supply responsiveness to any given increase in demand.

Summary

In comparison with the post-1979 record of other OECD countries, Norway stands out in combining a very favourable employment performance, witnessed by high participation rates and very low unemployment, with only slightly above-average wage growth. The maintenance of low rates of unemployment throughout the 1970s and 1980s must be seen against the background of two specific features: first, the high priority traditionally being attached by successive Norwegian governments to the preservation of full employment, and secondly, the rapid development of the oil sector, which directly *via* its claims on Mainland resources and indirectly *via* the distribution of its oil rent to the Mainland sectors represented a powerful source of demand stimulus, freeing, at the same time, the economy from balance-of-payments and budgetary constraints. A number of positive features of the past labour market record, and in particular the exceptionally low equilibrium unemployment rate, can however also be credited to institutional features, notably the high degree of unionisation and the relative strength of central bargaining units of the two sides of industry. Wages appear to be very sensitive to the state of the labour market, at least over the range experienced in the past. A notable feature is that flexibility is primarily provided at the central level and apparently not through wagedrift which in Norway is taken to include collective settlements at the local level. This highlights the importance of bargaining between federations of unions and employers and raises the issue of the appropriate roles of both central and local collective bargaining. Governments through their active and permanent participation in the institutionalised consensus-building process have played an important role in moderating wage claims during most of the period reviewed. The inclusion of the Government as a third party in the bargaining process itself proved to be disappointing in the 1970s, and there is little evidence that attempts to influence wages through tax and other concessions have met with great success. However, in the event of serious bargaining deadlocks, temporary recourse to administrative or legislative wage regulation has also produced favourable results. With respect to the present rebalancing problem, perhaps the most important message which could be derived from the available empirical work is that no single or collective action by the three principal labour market parties to moderate wage inflation and thereby to strengthen the foreign balance seems likely to succeed in the presence of excess demand pressure in the labour market.

V. Conclusions

Progress towards correcting imbalances in the economy continued in 1988. Improvements in the external balance exceeded expectations and the deceleration of inflation appears to have gathered momentum more recently. Under the impact of tight economic policies and reduced dissaving of households, domestic demand and imports fell for the second consecutive year. As export markets expanded strongly, the current external deficit of the Mainland economy declined markedly, despite weak international cost competitiveness. The objective of bringing inflation into line with trends in trading partner countries has not yet been attained. A related unsatisfactory feature was that a significant shift of resources to exposed non-oil sectors does not seem to have taken place. The recent easing of labour market pressure, however, should favour compliance with income regulation, and thereby help improve the conditions for better external and internal balance of the economy.

Indeed, on present and announced policies, the process towards reducing macroeconomic imbalances can be expected to continue, though at a more moderate pace than hitherto: the decline in domestic demand is likely to peter out, while the deterioration in the competitive position may have come to a halt. Short-term employment considerations have induced the authorities to refrain from tightening policies further. In the light of some recent indicators, weaker-than-projected activity at the turn of 1988 and beyond cannot be excluded. The associated easing of pressures on resources would help prevent wage and price inflation from reaccelerating after the expiry of present income regulation in spring 1989. However, in major export firms profits have increased substantially and there is still excessive demand in some segments of the labour market. If these factors were allowed to strongly influence overall wage formation the adjustment process could clearly be put at risk.

Yet, even if this risk were to be successfully contained, the question arises whether stabilisation results would then be satisfactory. Despite the recent recovery in oil prices and increased oil production, the overall current external account may still be in deficit by some 2 per cent of GDP in 1989. This means that Norway is exhausting its oil wealth at a relatively rapid rate while accumulating foreign debt. The ensuing debt-servicing burden on future generations has to be weighed against the cost in terms of lost output and increased unemployment that would accompany a significantly more rapid adjustment path. In any case, given limited oil reserves and uncertainties as to whether oil can be replaced by gas, it would seem appropriate to save part of the accruing oil rents and to start running current account surpluses. These should be the higher, the faster the rate of natural resource depletion and the higher the level of export prices of oil and gas. To this end, a transfer of resources to the traditional exposed sectors of the economy has to get under way. As emphasised in previous Economic Surveys, this requires above all an *improvement* in competitiveness, a shift of profitability in favour of non-oil tradeables, curbs on public expenditure, notably transfers, and discouragement of excessive oil investment.

Contrary to what was expected in the aftermath of the oil-price collapse, oil investment will pick up strongly, spurred, *inter alia*, by tax changes. Oil output capacity has already risen by almost one-half since 1986. Last year's Survey underlined the importance of restraining the pace of oil development, as an increased weight of oil in the economy would run counter to the Government's strategy of strengthening traditional industries. Decisions already taken will entail a marked increase in investment and production capacity in the early 1990s. This will lead to higher imports of oil equipment and tend to increase demand pressure in the oil-dependent sectors of the Mainland economy. As such an expansion of the oil sector may not be avoidable, moderation in public expenditure growth seems all the more important.

Budgetary restraint pursued at the central government level has been in part offset by high deficit-spending of local authorities. Moreover, fiscal retrenchment has been achieved mainly through tax increases, with growth in public expenditure, notably transfers, continuing relatively strongly. Looking ahead, the central government budget for 1989 implies no change in the fiscal stance. In the face of high and rapidly-growing debt-revenue ratios the rise in local government deficits can be expected to be reversed, especially if provisions to control local government borrowing are implemented more effectively. The tax burden is likely to remain broadly unchanged in 1989. But the expenditure/GDP ratio, net of oil-related spending, may increase by as much as 2 percentage points, mainly reflecting rising transfers. Existing commitments in the field of social security put strong upward pressure on public spending. The impact of the ageing population on health and pension benefits is compounded by the maturing of the pension system. The "automatic" volume increase in public spending is estimated to be 2 per cent per year. In effect, discretionary measures, such as additional spending on labour market schemes in 1988/89, will make for an even higher rate.

Continued tight fiscal policy is also indispensable to maintain the credibility of the Government's medium-term strategy, helping avoid turbulence in the foreign-exchange market and reducing the risk premium demanded by the market for investing in Norwegian kroner. Since the devaluation in 1986 the authorities have used interest-rate policy to support the exchange rate. Securing net capital inflows sufficiently large to match current-account deficits has required high interest rates by international standards, contributing to the marked slowdown in credit expansion after several years of overshooting official targets. While tighter monetary conditions are consistent with the official strategy of rebalancing the economy, and of curbing the household sector's debt accumulation, it is crucial to the adjustment process that fixed investment in the exposed sector not be impeded by high financing costs. The liberalisation of firms' long-term borrowing in foreign currencies should contribute both to more stable capital inflows and lower financing costs. The decline in inflation rates has allowed a significant reduction in nominal interest rates over the past year and a substantial reduction of interest rate differentials *vis-à-vis* main trading partners. The scope for further cuts in interest rates is dependent upon a continuation of declining cost and price inflation which should strengthen market confidence in the rebalancing process.

The incomes policy approach of the Government, aimed at bringing cost increases into line with international developments and requirements of external balance without sacrificing employment objectives is a central element of the overall economic strategy. The existing institutional labour-market setting, of which the Government through its consultative bodies is an integral part, would seem to have contributed both to keeping the equilibrium rate of unemployment low as compared with other countries and to enhancing the responsiveness of wages to adverse supply shocks and changes in the level of unemployment. Even so, viewed against the marked disinflation process in main trading partner countries, Norway's labour cost performance over the 1980s has clearly been unsatisfactory.

Given the apparent sensitivity of centrally-negotiated wages to macroeconomic forces, it is arguable that the existence of more than one collective bargaining level might be partly responsible for excessive wage increases. It seems tempting therefore to seek to limit the role of local bargaining and other elements of wagedrift. Although wagedrift may have played an important role in the allocation of labour resources, local negotiators appear to be rather insensitive to the state of the *national* labour market and the economy's ability to pay, responding only to pressures in local markets and the business situation of their respective firms or branches of industry. In order to improve cost competitiveness, changes in the institutional set-up and wage bargaining process at both the central and the local level may be called for. Irrespective of the precise institutional arrangements, however, the authorities need to ensure that the wage determination system does not have to operate under excessive demand pressure.

The rise in relative costs in the 1980s must be seen against the background of high demand for labour during most of the period. How far pressures have to ease before the desired improvement in competitiveness can be brought about depends importantly on the responsiveness of the social partners. Higher efficiency growth in the exposed sector should contribute to an improvement in competitiveness, though the link between wages and productivity seems rather strong. Measures to damp consumer-price inflation via promotion of competition in the sheltered sector and lowering cost pressure would also assist the wage disinflation process in the exposed sector. Past experience suggests that attempts to influence wage trends by various concessions, such as tax reductions and extensions of social programmes, runs the risk of contributing to excessive demand for labour, thereby putting pressure on the wage-formation system. Direct income regulation measures, though continuing to represent an important option in the event of abrupt changes in the economic environment, should be of limited duration, given their interference with the resource allocation function of the wage system. Moreover, if used too frequently, their effectiveness would be compromised.

In summary, notwithstanding the progress made so far in unwinding economic imbalances, much remains to be done. A country like Norway, which is depleting a sizeable natural resource at a relatively fast rate, should aim at running current-account surpluses and step up its national saving ratio. The required transfer of resources from the domestically-oriented sectors of the economy has not yet occurred. To the extent that the prospective increase in private savings is not sufficient to improve the external debt position and, at the same time, match the financing needs of higher investment in the exposed sector, higher public saving would be required. For rebalancing the economy, two additional conditions must be met: a major improvement in international competitiveness and accompanying relative price and income shifts in favour of exposed non-oil activities.

Notes and references

1. See Table 6.1 in the OECD *Employment Outlook* 1987, Paris 1987.
2. See Table 1.3 in the OECD *Employment Outlook* 1987, Paris 1987.
3. Setting part-time employment equivalent to half of full-time employment, the adjusted participation rate in Norway in 1986 was 62½ per cent. The corresponding values were 66 per cent for Denmark, and 59½ per cent for Germany.
4. For Norway, see Table 2.52 in Norges Offentlige Utredninger, *Inntektsdannelsen i Norge* (NOU 1988:24), Oslo 1988; for other countries, see Chapter 3 in the OECD *Employment Outlook* 1988, Paris 1988.
5. See Table C.1 in the OECD *Employment Outlook* 1988, Paris 1988.
6. For a survey of empirical studies based on the traditional framework, see N.M. Stolen, "Faktorer bak Lonnsueksten", *Okonomiske Analyser* N° 9, Statistisk Sentralbyra, 1985. A recent comprehensive study along these lines is reported in Norges Offentlige Utredninger, *Inntektsdannelsen i Norge*, (NOU 1988:24), Oslo 1988. Studies based on the bargaining approach include M. Hoel and R. Nymoen, "Wage formation in Norwegian Manufacturing. An Empirical Application of a Theoretical Bargaining Model", *Arbeidsnotat* 5, Norges Bank 1986; S. Holden, "Wagedrift in Norway: A bargaining approach", *Memorandum* N° 20, Dept. of Economics, University of Oslo 1987; and K.N. Kjaer and A. Rodseth, "Wage formation in Norway. What can aggregate time series tell us?", *Memorandum* N° 6, Dept. of Economics, University of Oslo, 1987.
7. See O. Aukrust, "PRIM 1: A model of the price and income distribution mechanism of an open economy", *Artikler* 35, Central Bureau of Statistics, Oslo 1970; O. Aukrust, "Inflation in an open economy: a Norwegian model", in L.B. Krause and W.S. Salant (eds.): *Worldwide inflation: Theory and recent experience*, Brookings institution, Washington D.C., 1977. For an integration of the Scandinavian model and a bargaining model, see R. Nymoen, "Modelling wages in the small open economy. An error-correction model of Norwegian manufacturing wages", *Arbeidsnotat* 4, Norges Bank, 1988.
8. See L. Calmfors and J. Driffil, "Centralisation of wage bargaining and macroeconomic performance", *Economic Policy*, April 1988; and OECD *Economic Outlook* 43, Paris 1988.

Annex I

Theories of wage determination

The factors determining the wage formation process may be grouped into three broad categories: *market forces*, *efficiency wages* and *unions*. The first two are mainly relevant for wagedrift. Unions do not only play an important role in central wage settlements but also in local settlements, which statistically appear as wagedrift in Norway.

Market forces

The market-clearing wage equates demand and supply of labour. If a wage rate determined through central wage settlements is lower than the market-clearing wage, market forces tend to move it upwards towards equilibrium. The impact of these market forces is reflected in the wagedrift. In the extreme case, where the labour market is homogeneous and the wage rate is always at its market clearing level, total wage changes will be independent of central wage settlements.

In reality, the labour market is more or less segmented in different occupations, skills and regions. For each sub-market, there is a clearing wage at any time. Central wage settlements set a floor for the wage rate in each sub-labour market: where the equilibrium wage lies above the centrally-negotiated wage, forces of demand and supply will generate wagedrift; conversely, no wagedrift will develop in sub-markets with a market-clearing wage below the centrally-negotiated wage.

With heterogeneous labour, pure market theory combined with central wage settlements would predict that the wage in any sub-market always equals, whichever is higher, the market-clearing wage or the centrally-negotiated wage. Such a theory of wage determination would not contradict the empirical evidence of wagedrift being lower, and total wage increase being higher, the higher the centrally-negotiated wage. The reason for this property is that the average measured wage increase is an aggregate of wage growth in different parts of the labour market. In sub-markets where wages are equal to their market-clearing levels, wages are independent of the centrally-negotiated wage. On the other hand, wage inflation will be equal to the centrally-negotiated wage increases where the latter exceed the equilibrium wage. Aggregating over these different types of sub-markets gives a negative correlation between central wage settlements and wagedrift.

A pure market theory only predicts wagedrift in sectors with full employment or excess demand for labour. Unemployment will only occur in sectors where the wage is given by central wage settlements. Consequently, involuntary unemployment can occur only if unions force wages above their market-clearing levels through central bargaining.

Efficiency wages

Various modifications of the simplest textbook market theory make unemployment possible even in the absence of unions. An important departure is embodied in the *efficiency wage theory* (see e.g. Akerlof and Yellon (1986) or Yellon (1984) for an overview). According to this theory, wages are unilaterally set by individual firms. The reason why each firm does not set wages as low as possible is that the wage rate is assumed to have some positive effect on the firm's profit, thus giving an offset to the negative direct cost effect. Several reasons for such positive effects have been suggested: a high wage may increase workers' morale and effort (see e.g. Shapiro & Stiglitz (1984), Solow (1979) and Akerlof (1982)); it may reduce quit rates and thereby reduce training and turnover costs (Salop (1979) and Schlicht (1978)), and it may increase the quantity and quality of applicants for vacancies (Jackman, Layard and Pissarides (1984), Weiss (1980)).

Efficiency wage theory assumes that firms unilaterally set wages, balancing the negative cost effects of high wages against the positive effects. This leads to an equilibrium wage distribution, where wages may very well be above market-clearing levels in some or all segments of the labour market. Involuntary unemployment is thus possible in the absence of unions.

According to efficiency wage theory, the optimal wage rate for one firm will usually depend on wages in other firms. As long as some firms or sub-sectors have wages equal to centrally-negotiated wages, actual wages should depend on central settlements. In contrast to the simplest market theory of wages, it is now possible to have sectors registering unemployment and wagedrift simultaneously. Also, the total wage increase will be positively correlated to centrally-negotiated wage increases.

However, the distinction between the simple market theory and efficiency wage theory is not sharp. The introduction of labour turnover and of the number/quality of applicants for vacancies demonstrates that there is no sharply-defined market clearing wage. In the simplest market theory, a firm can get as much (homogeneous) labour as it wishes as long as its wage is equal to or above the market clearing level, while it will not get any labour at all if its wages are lower. Efficiency wage theory substitutes this extreme "all or nothing" property with the far more realistic alternative that the available amount and quality of labour to a firm is a rising function of its wage.

Unions

The behaviour of unions is obviously of significant importance for wage determination in Norway. This is true both for central wage settlements and for wagedrift, since wagedrift includes wage increases obtained through settlements between local unions and firms. During the last decade, there has been a vast amount of theoretical and empirical economic research on union behaviour, bargaining, etc. It usually assumes that the outcome of wage bargaining depends partly on the preferences of the union and partly on the relative bargaining strengths of unions and employers. Unions are usually assumed to care about unemployment as well as wages. Even if unions unilaterally set wages, and firms set employment, the unions' wage claims would be constrained by the employment consequences. The more a union cares about unemployment relative to wage increases, the closer will the union's desired wage be to the market-clearing wage.

The outcome of wage negotiations will depend on the bargaining strength of the two parties. Modern bargaining theory stresses the importance of possible deadlocks on the outcome. Usually it is assumed that the consequence of not reaching an agreement is a strike. Although a strike often is the consequence of not reaching an agreement under central wage negotiations, the same does not apply to local (firm level) wage negotiations in Norway. As mentioned in the main body of the Survey, LO and NAF have agreed not to use strikes and lockouts in local bargaining. These are, however, replaced by formal or informal "go slow" and "work to rule" actions (see Moene (1987) and Holden (1988) for analyses of wage bargaining in such an event).

Local wage bargaining with withdrawal of co-operation – and thereby reduced labour efficiency – has several similarities with efficiency wage theory. If wages are too low, efficiency wage theory assumes that workers spontaneously and individually act in a manner leading to lower efficiency (i.e. higher effective costs). A union threatening to withdraw co-operation in support of its wage claims confronts the firm with a similar situation. Another important link between the two theories is that high wage increases will have positive effects on profits: through improved efficiency in one case and through less cost of industrial strife in the other (see Hoel (1988a) for a more detailed analysis of this issue).

The outcome of wage bargaining will usually depend on the conditions in the labour market: market forces remain important if wages are determined through bargaining between unions and employers. This is true regardless of at which level bargaining takes place.

Labour demand and unemployment

The theories discussed above all suggest that wage inflation is influenced by the state of the labour market. According to the simple market force theory, an increase in aggregate demand for labour would put upward pressure on wages so as to equilibrate supply and demand. As for the efficiency wage theory, the positive effects of high wages are likely to rise with a tightening of labour markets: when there is strong competition among firms for labour, each firm may find it particularly profitable to increase its wage in order to reduce turnover and increase the number of applicants for vacancies. Once labour markets ease, there is less need to use high wages to retain workers. The state of the labour market also enters into union models, since unions are assumed to care about employment and wages. An increase in the demand for labour will make it possible for a union to achieve higher wages without adverse employment consequences. At the firm level, low aggregate unemployment will also make the union less concerned about the risk of members losing jobs at the firm, since employment possibilities will be good elsewhere. With low unemployment, unions will therefore be more aggressive in their wage demands.

In the literature, it has often been assumed that there is some "natural" rate of unemployment or "non-accelerating inflation rate of unemployment" (NAIRU). These "equilibrium" rates of unemployment may be defined precisely in various ways. The general idea, however, is that real wages will decline if unemployment is above the long-run equilibrium level. This in turn will make unemployment decline towards the long-run equilibrium level.

Recently, the notion of a stable "natural" rate of unemployment has been questioned. Studies for several countries indicate that high unemployment may only have a temporary damping effect on wages. This implies that it may be impossible to reduce unemployment from any level without getting inflationary pressure. Thus, the long-run rate of unemployment, which is consistent with a stable rate of inflation, depends on the history of the economy: the NAIRU or "natural" rate will increase after a period of high unemployment. This phenomenon is sometimes referred to as "hysteresis" in the literature.

One reason why high unemployment could only have a temporary damping effect on wages is that people who have been unemployed for a long period may become less active in their job search or less employable (see Nickell (1987)). After a while, therefore, the number of vacancies will increase in spite of continued high unemployment. Upward wage pressure related to market forces and efficiency wages may thus occur even if unemployment remains high. An alternative explanation is related to the unions' attitude towards employment. Unions are usually considerably more concerned about keeping their members (the "insiders") employed than creating employment opportunities for newcomers (the "outsiders", see Blanchard and Summers (1986)). If labour demand for some reason falls and union members become unemployed, the union will initially be concerned about the re-employment possibilities of these members. After a while, however, these members will lose their "insider status" and the union will be more occupied with improving the living standards of members still in employment.

High unemployment is often assumed to make individual unions more concerned about the dangers of their members losing jobs. However, as long as unemployment is *stable*, high unemployment does not necessarily imply poor employment prospects for a person recently laid-off. Since employers find workers who have been unemployed for some time less attractive than workers who have recently been employed, the latter group of workers can expect to find a new job rather easily in spite of high unemployment (see the evidence for the British labour market by Blanchard and Summers (1988)). With *rising* unemployment, however, there will be a larger flow into unemployment than out of unemployment. Even recently laid-off workers may find it difficult to find new employment in this situation. Thus, *rising* unemployment could have a dampening effect on wages, while the downward pressure may be considerably weaker when unemployment is high and stable.

Productivity and prices

All theories of wage determination suggest that higher productivity and higher producer prices should lead to higher wages. For the market force and efficiency wage theories, these factors affect wages through their impact on labour demand. In a bargaining context, unions' demand for wage increases will be influenced by an improvement in profits as a result of higher productivity and producer prices. Under most plausible assumptions about the outcome of the bargaining process, negotiated wages will be positively correlated with productivity and producer prices.

Consumer and producer prices are usually closely related. Nevertheless, it is useful to study the effect on wages of an isolated increase in consumer prices, for a given level of producer prices. (Such an isolated increase in consumer prices could e.g. be caused by an increase in import prices or in indirect taxes.) For a given level of disposable real income per worker, nominal wages must rise if consumer prices rise. Theoretical considerations suggest that an increase in consumer prices (for given producer prices) could have the same effect on nominal wages as a rise in income tax rates. The effect of income tax increases on wages is, however, theoretically ambiguous.

Taxes

The effect of a tax cut, which reduces both average and marginal tax rates, is ambiguous for all three factors of wage determination discussed above, i.e. market forces, efficiency wages and unions.

A tax cut will have two effects on labour supply if wages are determined by pure market forces: on the one hand, a lower (marginal) tax rate increases the return from working more, thus stimulating labour supply (substitution effect); on the other hand, a lower (average) tax rate increases the demand for both leisure and material goods, thus reducing labour supply (income effect). Only if the substitution effect dominates the income effect will a tax cut increase labour supply and lower equilibrium wages.

Similar ambiguity occurs if wages are determined by unions. If the (average) tax rate is reduced, the union can simultaneously increase the after-tax wage for its members and reduce unemployment by reducing pre-tax wages somewhat. This tends to reduce wages. A reduction in the (marginal) tax rate, on the other hand, increases the cost (in terms of foregone disposable income) of keeping unemployment low. This tends to make for higher wages in response to a tax cut. The net effect of a tax cut on the wage rate therefore remains ambiguous (see e.g. Oswald (1985)).

The same is true in the case of efficiency wages. Whether or not a tax cut will reduce wages depends both on how wages affect profits and on central parameter values (see Hoel (1988b) for a further analysis).

A reduced marginal tax rate combined with an unchanged average tax rate will increase labour supply, and thus reduce the market-clearing wage. In the context of efficiency wages and unions, on the other hand, the same type of tax reduction tends to *increase* the wage rate. Conversely, for reduced average taxes with unchanged marginal tax rates: the market-clearing wage will rise (due to reduced labour supply), while in most specifications of efficiency wage models or union models one will find that wages go down as a response to such a tax cut.

Average wages are determined through some combination of market forces, efficiency wage considerations, and union activity. Even for simple tax changes of the types discussed above (i.e. if only marginal taxes or only average taxes are reduced) the effects of the tax reduction on wages is uncertain.

References

Akerlof, G.A. (1982), "Labour contracts as a parital gift exchange", *Quarterly Journal of Economics* 87 (November), 543-69.

Akerlof, G.A. and Yellen, J.L., eds. (1986), *Efficiency wage models of the labour market*, Cambridge University Press.

Blanchard, O.J. and Summers, L.H. (1986), "Hysteresis and the European unemployment problem", in S. Fischer (ed.): *NBER Macroeconomics Annual 1986*, MIT Press, Cambridge, Massachusetts.

Blanchard, O.J. and Summers, L.H. (1986), "Beyond the natural rate hypothesis", *American Economic Review, Papers and Proceedings* 78, 182-87.

Hoel, M. (1987), "Endogen makrookonomisk politikk med fagforeninger", *Sosialokonomen* 7/87, 26-33.

Hoel, M. (1988a), "Efficiency wages and local versus central bargaining", Dept. of Economics, University of Oslo, Memorandum N° 7/88.

Hoel, M. (1988b), "Efficiency wages and income taxes", University of Munich.

Holden, S. (1987), "Wagedrift in Norway: A bargaining approach", Dept. of Economics, university of Oslo, Memorandum N° 20/87.

Jackman, R., Layard, R. and Pissarides, C. (1984), "On vacancies", London School of Economics, Centre for Labour Economics, Discussion Paper N° 165 (revised).

Moene, K. (1988), "Union threats and wage determination", *Economic Journal*, forthcoming.

Nickell, S. (1987), "Why is wage inflation in Britain so high?", *Oxford Bulletin of Economics and Statistics* 49 (N° 1).

Oswald, A.J. (1985): "The economic theory of trade unions: An introductory survey", *Scandinavian Journal of Economics* 87, 160-193.

Salop, S.C. (1979), "A model of the natural rate of unemployment", *American Economic Review* 69, 117-25.

Schlicht, E. (1978), "Labour turnover, wage structure and natural unemployment", *Zeitschrift für die gesamte Staatswissenschaft* 134, 337-46.

Shapiro, C. and Stiglitz, J.E. (1984), "Equilibrium unemployment as a worker discipline device", *American Economic Review"* 74 (June), 433-44.

Solow, R. (1979), "Another possible source of wage stickiness", *Journal of Macroeconomics* 1, 79-82.

Weiss, A. (1980), "Job queues and layoffs in layoffs in labour markets with flexible wages", *Journal of Political Economy* 88 (June), 526-38.

Yellon, J. (1984), "Efficiency wage models of unemployment", *American Economic Review, Papers and Proceedings* 74, 200-205.

Annex II

Calendar of main economic events

1987

January

Working hours per week were reduced from 40 to 37.5 hours with full compensation.

The Government decided to restrict oil production from February to June relative to production capacity. The loss in output is about 80 000 b/d.

The Bank of Norway lending rate was lowered from 14.8 to 14.5 per cent.

February

The Bank of Norway lending rate was lowered in two stages to 13.8 per cent.

March

The wage agreement between the traditional blue collar labour organisation (LO) and the employers' federation (NAF) resulted in a zero central wage settlement.

A Government White Paper on personal tax reform was presented to the Storting, recommending measures to broaden the tax base and to lower marginal tax rates.

The Government allocated eleven new blocks on the continental shelf to oil companies for exploration.

Construction of commercial buildings in the Oslo area was restricted until the end of the year to prevent overheating in the construction industry.

April

Wage settlements in the public sector were concluded with no central wage increases in 1987; the agreement was to be reviewed in January 1988 in the light of wage developments in the private sector during 1987.

June

The 1987 Revised National Budget was passed by the Storting; government provisions in some areas were cut to keep expenditures at the central level in line with the 1987 Budget; revised revenue projections pointed to a significant improvement in the central government financial balance.

The income settlement for farmers resulted in moderate increases.

Primary reserve requirements for banks and life insurance companies were abolished.

New Central Bank loan facilities were established for commercial banks to finance longer-term credit extensions.

Production restrictions on oil adopted in January were extended until the end of the year.

July

Financing companies were required to observe reserve requirements on a monthly basis.

October

The 1988 National Budget was presented to the Storting:
- The oil-adjusted central government budget balance was estimated to have been in surplus in 1987 but a small deficit was expected in 1988. Discretionary measures were proposed to increase taxes by about Kr. 3 billion; government outlays on goods and services and transfers to households were set to show continued rapid growth;
- The budget proposals included some reduction in the progressivity of central government income taxes, and a broadening of the tax base;
- The annual credit budget was to be replaced by a domestic credit growth target: for 1988 the target range was set at 8-12 per cent.

Supplementary reserve requirements on bank lending were abolished.

December

The 1988 Budget was passed by Parliament:
- The budget balance in 1988 was expected to improve by about Kr. 2½ billion compared to the draft proposal. This reflected revised tax estimates (Kr. ½ billion) and discretionary measures on both the income and outlay side of the budget (Kr. 2 billion).
- The oil-adjusted central government budget balance in 1988 was expected to show a surplus of Kr. 2.2 billion, and the overall surplus to be in the order of 2 per cent of GDP.

Limitations on building activity in the Oslo area were extended into the first half of 1988.

1988

January

The Government extended limitations on oil production to 7.5 per cent below potential for six months.

A review of public sector wages resulted in increases of Kr.2 500 per employee.

February

Agreement was reached for the new two-year settlement period between the traditional blue-collar labour organisation (LO) and the employers' federation (NAF). Main elements were:
- General wage increase of Kr.1 per hour;
- Special additional increase for groups with low incomes and for workers with particularly low wage increases in 1987;
- All local wage negotiations suspended during the first year of the agreement;
- Voluntary retirement at 66 as from 1989, and at 65 as from 1990.

The Government issued a decree, freezing wages and dividend payments while an income regulation law was being prepared.

March

The Income Regulation Act was passed by Parliament. The LO/NAF agreement served as a model for permissible wage increases for all workers until March 1989. Over the same period, dividend payments were limited to 12 per cent of the equity stock, or the highest dividend ratio in the last three years. The Act had special provisions for wages of teachers and nurses.

April

A committee set up to evaluate wage increases for teachers concluded that, in general, they should be moved up by one grade on the salary scale.

May

The Storting approved the first phase of a major new oil field (Snorre). It also approved the sale of state holdings in the oil field.

The Bank of Norway lending rate was lowered from 13.8 to 13.3 per cent.

June

The 1988 Revised National Budget was passed by the Storting; adjustments to the original budget projections mainly reflected lower estimated oil revenues and increased expenditure on oil activities.

The Bank of Norway lending rate was lowered to 12.8 per cent.

Restrictions on oil production were extended until the end of 1988.

July

Direct regulations on credit flows of non-bank financial institutions were abolished, as well as on bond emissions for housing purposes.

September

In response to the financial difficulties of the banking system, the Bank of Norway issued a statement saying that it would be ready to take any measures considered necessary to maintain trust in the banking system.

The Bank of Norway and the Guarantee Fund of the Commercial Banks intervened to rescue Norway's fifth largest bank.

October

The 1989 National Budget was presented to the Storting:
- The central government budget surplus was expected to rise from Kr. 2½ billion in 1988 to Kr. 5 billion in 1989; the deficit in the oil-adjusted central government budget was estimated to increase from ½ per cent of Mainland GDP in 1988 to 1¼ per cent in 1989. Government outlays on goods and services and transfers to households were set to show continued rapid growth; the tax burden was expected to remain broadly unchanged;
- The domestic credit growth target range for 1989 was set at 5 to 9 per cent.

The Bank of Norway lending rate was reduced to 12.4 per cent.

December

The Bank of Norway lending rate was reduced to 12 per cent.

The 1989 Budget was passed by Parliament:
- The projected overall deficit increased by about Kr. 3¾ billion compared to the draft proposal, reflecting both revised income estimates (Kr. 2 billion) and outlay estimates (Kr. 1¾ billion).
- The central government budget balance, adjusted for items related to oil activity and transfers from the Bank of Norway, was expected to show a deficit of Kr. 8¼ billion.
- The turnover tax on shares was suspended.
- A new venture capital company was established, jointly owned by the central government (49 per cent) and the private sector (51 per cent).

STATISTICAL ANNEX

Table A. **Supply and use of resources**
Kr. million, current prices

	1978	1979	1980	1981	1982	1983	1984	1985	1986	1987
Consumers' expenditure on goods and services	110 670	120 104	135 241	155 205	175 310	192 979	210 921	245 439	278 764	294 796
General government current expenditure on goods and services	43 543	46 585	53 478	62 616	70 408	78 213	84 099	92 654	102 005	116 325
Defence	6 354	6 784	8 018	10 227	11 141	12 547	12 987	14 416	15 286	18 191
Civil	37 009	39 801	45 460	52 389	59 267	65 666	71 112	78 238	86 719	98 134
Gross fixed capital formation	67 705	66 186	70 798	91 793	92 262	103 447	117 567	110 042	146 133	156 212
Change in stocks	−6 941	−460	8 104	−7 761	3 809	−4 332	−1 300	11 103	5 515	1 654
National expenditure	214 977	232 415	267 621	301 853	341 789	370 307	411 287	459 238	532 417	568 987
Exports of goods and services (non-factor)	87 221	105 407	134 795	156 288	165 023	183 921	214 077	235 564	194 629	199 731
Imports of goods and services (non-factor)	89 119	99 154	117 371	130 467	144 543	152 031	172 852	194 602	212 469	211 794
Gross domestic product in purchasers' values	213 079	238 668	285 045	327 674	362 269	402 197	452 512	500 200	514 577	556 924
Indirect taxes	37 946	41 106	49 024	55 696	61 747	69 733	78 200	91 037	99 795	104 710
Subsidies	16 446	16 743	19 960	21 795	23 662	24 439	25 709	26 936	29 569	30 777
Gross domestic product at factor cost	191 579	214 305	255 981	293 773	324 184	356 903	400 021	436 099	444 351	482 991
Depreciation and other operating provisions	34 598	36 878	41 358	48 053	55 007	59 614	62 512	66 512	72 707	81 429
Net domestic product at factor cost	156 981	177 427	214 623	245 720	269 177	297 289	337 509	369 587	371 644	401 562

Source: National Accounts.

Table B. **Supply and use of resources**
Kr. million

	1979	1980	1980	1981	1982	1983	1984	1985	1986	1986	1987
	1975 prices					1980 prices				1986 prices	
Consumers' expenditure on goods and services	84 389	91 488	135 241	136 784	139 199	141 303	145 139	160 171	169 862	278 764	272 597
General government current expenditure on goods and services											
Defence	35 277	37 191	53 478	56 763	58 985	61 727	63 238	65 358	67 398	102 005	105 813
Civil	5 133	5 450	8 018	9 236	9 289	9 895	10 009	10 476	10 659	15 287	16 920
Gross fixed capital formation	30 144	31 741	45 460	47 527	49 696	51 832	53 229	54 882	56 739	86 718	88 893
Change in stocks	48 912	48 181	70 798	83 485	74 296	78 618	87 224	68 883	87 452	146 133	142 677
	-649	4 344	8 104	-7 024	3 041	-3 108	-51	10 157	7 182	5 515	914
National expenditure	172 929	181 204	267 621	270 008	275 521	278 540	295 550	304 569	331 894	532 417	522 001
Exports of goods and services (non-factor)	79 724	81 392	134 795	136 651	136 451	146 786	158 841	175 758	176 859	194 629	195 302
Imports of goods and services (non-factor)	71 954	74 298	117 371	119 113	123 467	123 449	135 177	143 898	157 647	212 469	198 149
Gross domestic product in purchasers' values	180 699	188 298	285 045	287 546	288 505	301 877	319 214	336 429	351 106	514 577	519 154
Depreciation and other operating provisions	27 691	28 625	41 358	43 656	44 772	46 244	48 191	49 175	51 275	72 708	..
Net domestic product at market prices	153 008	159 673	243 687	243 890	243 732	255 633	271 023	287 255	299 831	441 869	..

Source: National accounts.

Table C. **Gross domestic product by origin**
Kr. million, current prices

	1977	1978	1979	1980	1981	1982	1983	1984	1985	1986	1987
Agriculture, forestry and fishing	9 467	9 815	10 136	10 969	12 957	13 437	13 135	15 042	15 150	16 714	19 348
Crude petroleum and natural gas production	7 771	13 737	22 367	43 140	52 552	57 913	69 361	85 870	92 693	55 626	56 188
Pipeline transport	407	950	1 613	2 149	2 573	2 566	2 506	2 483	2 987	5 604	5 863
Mining and quarrying	923	969	1 034	1 087	1 207	1 167	1 376	1 391	1 303	1 409	1 387
Manufacturing	35 963	37 528	43 820	45 635	48 575	51 383	56 724	64 524	70 127	75 073	82 996
Electricity supply	5 083	6 491	7 486	8 237	10 165	11 645	13 898	16 127	17 797	19 155	22 138
Construction	12 476	14 020	13 987	15 392	16 458	18 615	19 975	20 591	23 221	28 178	34 574
Wholesale and retail trade	21 662	23 892	24 882	30 115	34 697	38 372	40 328	43 668	47 928	54 720	59 616
Hotels and restaurants	2 278	2 609	2 803	3 148	3 779	4 393	5 147	5 777	6 599	7 446	8 780
Water transport and oil drilling	8 306	9 134	10 116	12 327	14 913	13 984	13 498	14 870	13 753	12 016	8 596
Other transport	10 968	12 115	12 653	13 795	16 483	18 834	21 722	23 486	25 084	30 060	32 631
Financing and insurance	5 935	6 654	7 653	8 991	11 749	14 402	15 931	15 105	16 625	23 784	24 562
Business services	5 761	6 409	8 086	9 186	10 797	13 054	14 701	17 557	21 652	25 202	29 034
Real estate	7 564	8 247	8 991	10 067	11 609	13 402	15 001	16 656	18 105	19 596	21 599
Other private services	9 905	10 929	11 625	12 798	14 281	16 057	18 114	19 195	21 889	25 028	28 528
Community, social and personal services	28 519	32 013	34 114	38 901	45 162	51 506	56 841	61 808	67 965	75 345	85 337
Other correction items	18 546	17 567	17 302	19 108	19 717	21 540	23 939	28 362	37 322	39 622	35 747
Gross domestic product in purchasers' values	191 534	213 079	238 668	285 045	327 674	362 270	402 197	452 512	500 200	514 578	556 924

Source: National accounts.

Table D. **Gross domestic product by industry of origin**
Kr. million

	1980	1981	1982	1983	1984	1984	1985	1986	1986	1987
		1980 prices					1984 prices			1986 prices
Agriculture, forestry and fishing	10 969	11 959	12 446	12 319	13 356	15 042	13 682	13 263	16 714	17 990
Crude petroleum and natural gas production	43 140	41 262	41 597	48 666	56 101	85 870	89 364	95 210	55 626	62 875
Pipeline transport	2 149	1 871	1 935	2 004	2 143	2 483	2 842	4 763	5 604	6 276
Mining and quarrying	1 087	1 106	1 056	1 204	1 183	1 391	1 293	1 403	1 409	1 317
Manufacturing	45 635	45 191	44 887	44 555	47 113	64 524	66 893	67 126	75 073	76 029
Electricity supply	8 237	8 959	9 096	10 291	10 619	16 127	15 660	15 326	19 155	20 541
Construction	15 392	15 124	15 506	16 046	16 093	20 591	21 724	23 690	28 178	29 013
Wholesale and retail trade	30 115	29 521	29 100	29 032	30 539	43 668	47 388	52 285	54 720	52 087
Hotels and restaurants	3 148	2 999	2 807	2 791	2 811	5 777	6 275	6 384	7 446	7 898
Water transport and oil drilling	12 327	12 784	11 981	11 961	12 799	14 870	14 520	13 972	12 016	8 545
Other transport	13 975	14 502	14 139	14 700	15 234	23 486	24 608	26 863	30 060	30 990
Financing and insurance	8 991	9 328	9 317	9 057	9 047	15 105	16 160	17 670	23 784	25 450
Business services	9 186	9 630	10 136	10 253	11 203	17 557	20 077	21 552	25 202	26 513
Real estate	10 067	10 352	10 756	10 963	11 243	16 656	17 180	17 611	19 596	20 435
Other private services	12 798	12 776	12 940	13 269	13 179	19 195	20 542	21 561	25 028	25 867
Community, social and personal services	38 901	41 141	43 393	44 993	46 248	61 808	63 768	65 071	75 345	77 046
Other correction items	18 928	19 041	17 412	19 773	20 303	28 362	34 405	32 736	39 622	30 281
Gross domestic product in purchasers' values	285 045	287 546	288 504	301 877	319 214	452 512	476 381	496 486	514 578	519 153

Source: National accounts.

Table E. **General government income and expenditure (new SNA)**
Kr. million

	1982	1983	1984	1985	1986	1987[1]
Current revenue	190 050	210 246	241 792	278 245	289 984	310 013
Indirect taxes	61 747	69 733	78 200	91 037	99 795	104 710
Social security contributions	43 494	47 149	50 511	57 314	67 426	78 111
Direct taxes	70 604	76 722	87 636	100 600	79 286	84 167
Income from interest	13 218	15 085	20 552	24 780	33 290	39 959
Other income	987	1 557	4 893	4 514	10 187	3 066
Current expenditure	165 599	184 179	198 580	217 823	244 423	275 789
Purchase of goods and services	70 409	78 213	84 099	92 654	102 006	116 326
Defence	11 141	12 547	12 987	14 439	15 325	17 448
Civi	59 268	65 666	71 112	78 215	86 681	98 878
Subsidies	23 662	24 439	25 709	26 936	29 569	30 777
Interest on the public debt	11 529	13 414	15 018	17 393	22 324	24 073
Current transfers	57 787	66 062	71 787	78 029	86 472	96 725
To households, etc.	54 516	62 212	67 917	73 819	81 525	91 503
To the rest of the world	3 271	3 850	3 870	4 210	4 947	5 222
Other expenditure	2 212	2 051	1 967	2 811	4 052	7 888
Net current saving	24 451	26 067	43 212	60 422	45 561	34 224
Depreciation and other operating provisions	2 979	3 186	3 339	3 840	4 210	4 805
Gross saving	27 430	29 253	46 551	64 262	49 771	39 029
Gross fixed capital formation	11 525	12 410	12 858	13 289	16 078	18 808
Net lending	15 905	16 843	33 693	50 973	33 693	20 221
Memorandum item:						
Revenue from oil sector	29 248	35 723	43 465	50 535	17 816	14 165

1. Preliminary estimates.
Source: National accounts.

Table F. **Production by sector**

Mining and manufacturing
Industrial production[1], 1980 = 100

	By sector of production			By destination			
	Total	Oil and gas	Manufacturing	Exports	Consumption	Investment	Input in building and construction	Other input
1977	81	42	101	76	100	138	103	89
1978	89	68	99	86	101	133	108	83
1979	96	81	102	92	102	135	104	93
1980	100	100	100	100	100	100	100	100
1981	99	96	99	98	100	197	103	91
1982	99	97	99	99	99	117	102	100
1983	108	114	98	109	100	116	104	98
1984	118	131	104	119	102	168	104	101
1985	121	138	106	122	104	180	108	103
1986	126	147	108	126	104	182	113	103
1987	135	164	110	135	107	183	114	108

1. Averages of monthly figures.
Sources: Central Bureau of Statistics, *Monthly Bulletin of Statistics*; *Statistisk Ukehefte*.

Table G. **Labour market and employment**

	Labour market					Employment						
	Registered un-employment	Jobs vacant[1]	1 000 man-years			Employees (1 000 persons)						
			Self em-ployed	Employees	Total	Agricul-ture, for-estry fishing	Mining and manu-facturing	Building and construction	Commerce	Maritime trans-port, other transport and communica-tions	Public adminis-tration	Other
	1 000 persons	Thousands										
1975	19.6	6.0	238	1 358	1 707	159	423	147	238	158	85	497
1976	19.9	6.7	235	1 389	1 789	168	426	148	264	161	92	530
1977	16.1	8.8	232	1 425	1 824	165	419	156	274	171	89	550
1978	20.0	7.0	231	1 444	1 854	161	408	163	277	170	91	584
1979	24.1	6.2	231	1 455	1 872	161	397	151	277	172	92	622
1980	22.3	8.0	230	1 484	1 908	159	414	142	320	174	101	593
1981	28.4	6.5	225	1 496	1 935	159	412	146	330	175	100	609
1982	41.4	5.0	222	1 497	1 943	154	399	147	331	183	103	624
1983	63.5	3.3	221	1 488	1 945	148	376	147	336	172	114	648
1984	66.6	4.3	218	1 507	1 970	143	387	148	330	176	117	665
1985	51.4	5.8	218	1 554	2 014	147	389	151	346	175	128	673
1986	36.2	10.5	226	1 607	2 086	151	401	155	364	179	142	689
1987	32.4	12.4	..	..	2 126	139	399	166	375	178	155	709

1. Averages of number of unfilled vacancies at the end of the month.
Sources: Central Bureau of Statistics, *Monthly Bulletin of Statistics*, and *Statistisk Ukehefte*.

Table H. **Balance of payments**
National accounts basis
Kr. million

	1980	1981	1982	1983	1984	1985	1986	1987
Goods and services								
Exports, total	137 495	156 288	165 022	183 921	214 078	235 563	194 629	199 731
Commodities	92 863	106 889	114 798	133 249	156 822	173 254	136 002	144 945
Crude petroleum and natural gas from the North Sea	41 399	48 087	53 472	63 844	78 328	85 380	53 077	53 620
Direct exports in connection with oil activity[1]	443	1 643	378	392	1 796	357	260	206
Other commodities	47 194	52 397	53 459	61 053	70 386	76 183	71 194	81 026
Ships and oil platforms	3 827	4 772	7 490	7 959	6 311	11 410	11 472	10 094
New	1 402	668	2 291	2 491	926	1 134	953	1 150
Second-hand	2 425	4 104	5 199	5 468	5 385	10 276	10 519	8 944
Services	41 932	49 390	50 224	50 672	57 256	62 309	58 627	54 787
Gross receipts in connection with shipping and oil drilling	27 745	32 551	31 141	31 226	35 877	38 199	32 891	27 195
Travel	3 716	4 430	4 727	4 910	5 388	6 493	7 836	8 387
Other services	7 686	8 892	10 803	11 097	12 566	13 594	14 113	15 009
Other oil activity	2 785	3 517	3 554	3 439	3 425	4 024	3 787	4 195
Imports, total	117 371	130 469	144 543	152 031	172 852	194 602	212 469	211 794
Commodities	84 543	90 516	100 458	102 520	116 542	133 927	153 072	151 580
Direct imports in connection with oil activity	828	745	672	4 057	3 197	1 164	1 278	1 827
Other commodities	82 281	84 895	91 573	91 776	107 770	127 512	145 932	143 660
Ships and oil platforms	1 434	4 876	8 213	6 687	5 575	5 251	5 862	6 093
New	1 108	4 141	7 718	6 334	4 667	4 555	5 435	3 349
Second-hand	326	735	495	353	908	696	427	2 744
Services	32 828	39 953	44 085	49 510	56 311	60 675	59 397	60 214
Gross expenditures in connection with shipping and oil drilling	16 532	19 145	19 831	19 968	23 871	26 580	23 097	20 666
Direct imports in connection with other oil activity	1 622	3 031	2 949	5 671	6 506	3 793	2 111	3 117
Travel	6 486	8 470	10 583	11 586	12 143	14 812	18 582	20 599
Other services	8 188	9 309	10 721	12 285	13 791	15 491	15 607	15 841
Net goods and services	17 424	25 820	20 480	31 890	41 225	40 961	-17 839	-12 063
of which:								
Selected items in connection with shipping[2]	11 706	10 905	9 359	10 287	11 665	17 568	18 727	14 884
Selected items in connection with oil activity[3]	41 932	49 092	55 011	60 190	74 923	85 591	48 583	49 173

Interest and transfers, net	-11 976	-13 360	-16 334	-17 245	-17 297	-14 280	-15 072	-15 516
From abroad, total	6 077	9 756	11 888	11 671	14 859	19 642	21 573	22 490
Interest and dividends	5 321	8 740	10 727	10 393	13 509	18 227	20 266	21 007
Transfers	756	1 016	1 161	1 278	1 350	1 415	1 307	1 483
To abroad, total	18 053	23 116	28 222	28 916	32 157	33 922	36 646	38 006
Interests and dividends	14 841	19 319	23 431	23 394	26 651	27 733	29 438	29 967
Transfers	3 212	3 796	4 971	5 522	5 506	6 189	7 208	8 039
Current Balance	5 448	12 460	4 146	14 645	23 929	26 682	-32 912	-27 579
Long-term capital, net	-4 094	-4 292	2 686	-10 755	18	-12 500	21 606	5 487
Official	-2 215	-5 419	-8 348	-12 363	-7 546	-1 908	6 487	3 043
Financial institutions	858	47	873	1 989	4 156	8 778	17 430	13 635
Shipping companies	-274	2 164	4 059	2 493	3 289	-1 799	-4 153	-2 146
Direct investment	-963	2 876	699	-156	-6 205	-14 732	-3 319	-4 821
Other	-1 500	-2 666	7 540	-1 291	-617	-1 583	2 030	1 119
Basic Balance	1 354	8 348	6 832	3 890	23 947	18 072	-11 306	-22 092
SDR allocations	199	206	–	–	–	–	–	–
Various adjustements and items not included in								
international reserves	2 704	-5 920	-14 123	-9 474	9 265	-7 787	9 190	-1 389
Short-term capital transactions, excl. Norges Bank	3 089	3 913	14 905	-13 763	2 849	11 764	-12 301	20 001
Change in Norges Bank's total foreign assets	7 346	6 547	7 614	-399	34 539	22 049	-14 417	-3 480
Memorandum item:								
Norges Bank's international reserves, level, end of								
period	31 315	36 581	48 751	51 272	85 444	111 998	97 011	93 122

1. Including adjustments owing to the distribution of investment expenditures in respect of oil fields developed in co-operation with United Kingdom.
2. Including net freight earnings from shipping, exports of second-hand ships and imports of ships.
3. Including exports of crude petroleum and natural gas, pipeline services, net receipts from oil drilling and second-hand oil platforms; imports of oil platforms and commodities and services direct to the North Sea.

Sources: Central Bureau of Statistics, *National Accounts 1960-1986*, and *Statistisk Ukehefte*.

Table I. **Foreign trade, total and by area**
$ million, monthly rates

	Imports, cif								Exports, fob							
	Total	OECD countries			Non-OECD countries				Total	OECD countries			Non-OECD countries		
		Total	OECD Europe		Comecon	OPEC	Others			Total	OECD Europe		Comecon	OPEC	Others
			EEC	Others							EEC	Others			
1977	1 072.8	923.2	486.2	261.8	32.9	44.5	72.7	726.0	585.6	411.9	130.2	23.6	19.3	97.4
1978	951.9	816.7	428.1	245.3	26.6	39.4	69.1	836.6	699.5	513.5	125.0	27.2	16.3	93.7
1979	1 143.9	997.0	539.2	290.9	33.2	35.0	78.7	1 121.1	969.6	732.1	167.8	21.6	21.2	108.7
1980	1 413.0	1 236.2	677.8	331.4	30.8	47.4	98.6	1 541.0	1 376.1	1 112.3	194.7	22.6	34.6	107.7
1981	1 301.7	1 166.6	602.7	306.1	33.1	21.5	80.4	1 494.0	1 331.2	1 066.8	184.1	22.1	28.9	111.8
1982	1 287.7	1 134.4	584.5	313.0	47.7	12.4	93.2	1 462.1	1 301.5	1 062.9	177.1	17.8	22.8	120.0
1983	1 123.9	997.7	508.6	281.3	40.4	9.9	75.8	1 498.7	1 358.1	1 053.0	204.6	18.3	21.5	100.7
1984	1 155.0	1 020.5	526.7	285.3	41.7	9.1	83.6	1 574.3	1 430.5	1 113.5	201.6	13.6	11.4	118.8
1985	1 291.2	1 156.8	611.7	318.7	36.0	11.4	87.0	1 659.3	1 472.0	1 152.7	202.6	14.5	10.6	162.3
1986	1 690.9	1 543.4	847.1	425.1	30.6	8.6	108.4	1 508.4	1 296.6	977.0	206.2	14.5	12.7	184.6
1987	1 881.3	1 685.8	933.5	493.4	37.1	7.4	151.1	1 790.2	1 575.4	1 152.1	276.1	18.6	11.6	184.6

Source: OECD, *Foreign Trade Statistics, Series A.*

Table J. Prices and wages

	Consumer prices, 1979 = 100			Wholesale prices, 1981 = 100				Average hourly earnings Kroner	
		of which:						Industry	
	Total	Food	Rent, heating and light	Total	Consumer goods	Investment goods	Input	Males	Females
1976	80.9	84	78	65	65	74	68	30.44[1]	24.16
1977	88.2	91	85	69	70	78	74	33.77	26.96
1978	95.4	96	94	72	75	83	77	36.44	29.24
1979	100.0	100	100	78	79	88	81	37.47	30.15
1980	110.9	109	112	90	89	95	91	40.97	33.55
1981	126.0	127	127	100	100	100	100	45.14	37.29
1982	140.3	145	143	106	109	105	107	49.76	41.42
1983	152.1	156	157	113	116	110	113	53.96	45.35
1984	161.6	167	169	120	124	114	119	58.59	49.15
1985	170.8	178	179	126	131	119	124	63.28	52.85
1986	183.1	194	188	129	138	127	132	69.69	58.40
1987	199.1	209	202	137	147	135	143	81.00[2]	67.83

1. From 1.4.1976 the number of normal weekly working hours has been reduced from 42.5 to 40.
2. From 1.1.1987 the number of normal weekly working hours has been reduced from 40 to 37.5.

Source: Central Bureau of Statistics, Monthly Bulletin of Statistics.

Table K. Money and credit (Kr. million)

Changes in money supply

	Government income surplus[1] and loan transactions, state banks and Central Bank	Commercial[2] Banks	Domestic liquidity supply	Foreign transactions	Change in broad money
1977	15 780	12 596	28 376	−11 713	16 663
1978	17 526	5 915	23 440	−10 005	13 435
1979	18 067	9 478	27 703	−9 084	18 619
1980	16 743	11 366	28 709	−9 872	18 837
1981	17 536	16 591	33 527	−13 721	19 806
1982	19 715	12 382	32 097	−12 063	20 034
1983	15 599	13 735	31 842	−12 049	19 793
1984	18 949	32 259	50 598	−5 062	45 536
1985	10 566	63 677	73 301	−31 572	41 729
1986	6 384	50 652	60 101	−45 626	14 475
1987	27 326	86 187	91 914	−38 535	53 379

Domestic lending by financial institutions — End of period

	Total[3]	Central Bank	Commercial banks	Savings banks	State Banks	Insurance companies	Mortgage credit institutions	Private financial institutions	Postal savings banks
1977	157 903	5 492	38 749[4]	30 463[4]	52 653	11 434	19 465	4 162	1 983
1978	179 793	2 139	41 653	33 362	64 394	12 538	21 776	5 103	2 345
1979	203 797	1 188	45 691	37 700	75 944	13 570	25 027	5 375	2 722
1980	227 020	814	49 986	41 882	86 454	14 585	29 537	5 590	2 884
1981	255 670	2 064	56 589	47 792	94 330	16 080	35 536	6 724	3 074
1982	286 968	1 882	63 169	53 307	101 925	18 542	41 337	9 975	3 648
1983	320 544	3 652	70 253	59 958	108 357	22 580	48 087	12 450	4 090
1984	375 703	1 542	89 288	75 614	116 650	27 401	53 534	15 467	4 557
1985	448 984	4 147	116 633	100 231	121 793	34 465	61 200	20 458	4 993
1986	534 609	69 835	143 783	123 937	129 559	44 983	76 955	32 206	5 460
1987	651 440	74 687	179 478	153 236	137 412	55 690	110 185	30 452	6 047

1. Excluding oil taxes.
2. Including tax-free allocations to funds and saving with tax reductions.
3. Breakdown does not add up total.
4. From 31.1. 1977 all receipts and expenditure are gross figures.

Sources: Central Bureau of Statistics, *Monthly Bulletin of Statistics*; Central Bank, *Economic Bulletin*.

Domestic credit by borrowing sector — End of period

	(1) Municipalities	(2) Business Total	of which: Agriculture, Fishing	of which: Mining and manufacturing	(3) Wage earners	Sum (1)+(2)+(3)
1977	15 414	70 895	9 219	25 913	74 699	161 005
1978	19 915	80 879	10 814	29 229	82 605	183 399
1979	26 530	88 668	12 387	31 346	92 159	207 357
1980	30 507	94 564	13 855	32 782	105 617	230 688
1981	33 083	106 704	15 557	35 613	119 726	259 513
1982	35 399	115 489	17 140	37 010	139 907	290 789
1983	38 869	128 541	18 612	40 185	153 468	320 878
1984	42 479	148 623	21 520	46 463	191 412	382 514
1985	..	..	22 820	45 910	231 028	455 360
1986	..	..	26 725	48 692	277 046	514 450
1987	..	..	..	..	341 562	657 571

The security market — During period

	Bond issues Domestic and foreign currency	Share issues
1977	22 400	1 625
1978	25 485	1 730
1979	24 735	1 685
1980	22 580	2 749
1981	23 235	2 014
1982	24 598	2 385
1983	39 687	3 141
1984	35 957	4 963
1985	52 777	8 111
1986	93 724	9 090
1987	64 657	

Gold and foreign exchange holdings ($ mill. end of period)

	Total	of which: Official (including IMF position)	of which: Commercial and savings banks
1977	1 820	1 592	94
1978	2 628	2 720	−214
1979	3 642	4 064	−753
1980	5 198	7 517	−2 319
1981	5 561	7 271	−1 710
1982	6 167	8 386	−2 219
1983	5 402	8 159	−2 757
1984	7 239	10 423	−3 184
1985	9 159	14 571	−5 412
1986	..	..	..
1987	..	..	..

Sources: Central Bureau of Statistics, *Monthly Bulletin of Statistics*; Central Bank, *Economic Bulletin*; IMF, *International Financial Statistics* and OECD, *Main Economic Indicators*.

BASIC STATISTICS

BASIC STATISTICS :

INTERNATIONAL COMPARISONS

	Units	Reference period[1]	Australia	Austria
Population				
Total	Thousands	1987	16 249	7 575
Inhabitants per sq.km	Number		2	90
Net average annual increase over previous 10 years	%		1.4	0.0
Employment				
Total civilian employment (TCE)[2]	Thousands	1987	7 079	32 997
of which: Agriculture	% of TCE		5.8	8.6
Industry	% of TCE		26.6	37.7
Services	% of TCE		67.6	53.7
Gross domestic product (GDP)				
At current prices and current exchange rates	Billion US$	1987	193.7	117.2
Per capita	US$		11 919	15 470
At current prices using current PPP's[3]	Billion US$	1987	204.9	88.4
Per capita	US$		12 612	11 664
Average annual volume growth over previous 5 years	%	1987	3.7	1.8
Gross fixed capital formation (GFCF)	% of GDP	1987	23.8	22.6
of which: Machinery and equipment	% of GDP		11.5 (86)	9.7
Residential construction	% of GDP		4.7 (86)	4.6 (86)
Average annual volume growth over previous 5 years	%	1987	1.7	2.3
Gross saving ratio[4]	% of GDP	1987	20.3	24.1
General government				
Current expenditure on goods and services	% of GDP	1987	18.2	19.0
Current disbursements[5]	% of GDP	1987	35.0 (86)	46.6 (86)
Current receipts	% of GDP	1987	34.7 (86)	47.9 (86)
Net official development assistance	% of GNP	1987	0.33	0.17
Indicators of living standards				
Private consumption per capita using current PPP's[3]	US$	1987	7 389	6 535
Passenger cars, per 1 000 inhabitants	Number	1985	..	306 (81)
Telephones, per 1 000 inhabitants	Number	1985	540 (83)	460 (83)
Television sets, per 1 000 inhabitants	Number	1985	..	300 (81)
Doctors, per 1 000 inhabitants	Number	1985	..	1.7 (82)
Infant mortality per 1 000 live births	Number	1985	9.2 (84)	11.0
Wages and prices (average annual increase over previous 5 years)				
Wages (earnings or rates according to availability)	%	1987	5.7	4.9
Consumer prices	%	1987	7.0	3.0
Foreign trade				
Exports of goods, fob*	Million US$	1987	26 484	27 084
as % of GDP	%		13.6	23.0
average annual increase over previous 5 years	%		4.4	11.6
Imports of goods, cif*	Million US$	1987	26 964	32 580
as % of GDP	%		13.9	27.7
average annual increase over previous 5 years	%		2.8	10.8
Total official reserves[6]	Million SDR's	1987	6 441	6 049
As ratio of average monthly imports of goods	Ratio		3.4	2.6

* At current prices and exchange rates.
1. Unless otherwise stated.
2. According to the definitions used in OECD *Labour force Statistics*.
3. PPP's = Purchasing Power Parities.
4. Gross saving = Gross national disposable income *minus* Private and Government consumption.
5. Current disbursements = Current expenditure on goods and services *plus* current transfers and payments of property income.
6. Gold included in reserves is valued at 35 SDR's per ounce. End of year.
7. Including Luxembourg.
8. Included in Belgium.
9. Including non-residential construction.

Spain	Sweden	Switzerland	Turkey	United Kingdom	United States	Yugoslavia
38 830	8 399	6 610	52 010	56 890	243 915	23 410
77	19	160	67	232	26	90
0.7	0.2	0.5	2.2	0.1	1.0	0.8
11 370	4 337	3 219 (86)	15 632 (86)	24 987	112 440	..
16.1	4.2	6.5	55.7	2.4	3.0	..
32.0	30.2	37.7	18.1	29.8	27.1	..
51.8	65.6	55.8	26.2	67.8	69.9	..
289.2	158.5	171.1	67.4	669.8	4 472.9	61.7 (86)
7 449	18 876	25 848	1 296	11 765	18 338	2 652 (86)
337.1	115.7	104.9	220.9	702.5	4 472.9	..
8 681	13 771	15 842	4 247	12 340	18 338	..
2.9	2.4	2.3	6.0	3.2	4.3	
20.7	19.0	25.2	24.5	17.3	17.3	21.6 (86)
6.4 (86)	8.5 (86)	8.8	8.6 (84)	8.1 (86)	7.6	..
4.0 (86)	3.8 (86)	16.4 (9)	2.7 (84)	3.8 (86)	5.0	..
3.8	3.6	6.0	7.3	4.7	7.0	..
21.9	18.0	31.7	24.1	17.2	14.7	..
14.4	26.7	12.8	9.1	20.9	18.6	14.3 (86)
36.1 (86)	60.0 (86)	30.1	..	42.9 (86)	35.5 (86)	..
35.0 (86)	61.6 (86)	34.5	..	41.6 (86)	31.2 (86)	..
0.06	0.88	0.31	..	0.28	0.20	..
5 521	7 273	9 349 *	2 844	7 731	12 232	1 335 (86)*
252	377	402	18 (82)	312 (83)	473 (84)	121 (83)
381 (86)	890 (83)	1 334	55 (83)	521 (84)	650 (84)	122 (83)
256 (82)	390	337	76 (79)	336 (84)	621 (80)	175 (83)
3.4 (86)	2.5	1.4 (84)	1.5 (83)	0.5 (83)	2.0 (85)	1.6 (82)
7.0 (84)	6.8	6.9	..	9.4	10.4 (86)	31.7 (83)
10.3	7.6	..	..	8.5	3.1	..
8.5	5.9	2.1	41.6	4.7	3.3	56.3
33 972	44 388	45 312	10 344	130 632	254 124	11 425
11.8	27.9	26.6	15.7	19.7	5.7	16.3
10.4	10.6	11.8	12.1	7.7	3.7	2.2
48 816	40 596	50 424	14 460	153 768	424 440	12 603
17.0	25.5	29.6	21.9	23.2	9.6	18.5
9.1	8.0	12.0	9.7	9.1	11.7	−3.1
22 035	5 974	22 283	1 254	30 070	33 657	557
6.4	2.1	6.3	1.2	2.8	1.1	0.6

23.1.89

Italy	Japan	Luxembourg	Netherlands	New Zealand	Norway	Portugal
57 331	122 091	372	14 671	3 284	4 184	10 280
190	328	143	432	12	13	112
0.3	0.7	0.3	0.6	0.5	0.3	0.5
20 584	59 110	164 (86)	5 135 (86)	1 517 (86)	2 090	4 156
10.5	8.3	3.7	4.9	10.5	6.7	21.9
32.6	33.8	32.9	25.5	28.9	27.0	35.8
56.8	57.9	63.4	69.6	60.6	66.3	42.3
758.1	2 376.5	6.0	213.2	35.1	82.7	36.7
13 224	19 465	16 138	14 530	10 620	19 756	3 761
702.5	1 609.4	5.5	179.7	35.3	64.5	61.4
12 254	13 182	14 705	12 252	10 680	15 405	6 297
2.6	3.9	4.0	2.1	2.1	4.1	2.1
19.9	28.9	22.6	20.3	21.2	28.0	25.3
10.0	10.5 (86)	9.0 (82)	10.0	13.1 (85)	7.9 (86)	14.7 (81)
5.2	5.0 (86)	4.7 (82)	5.2	4.6 (85)	5.0 (86)	6.4 (81)
2.8	5.3	0.8	4.8	2.0	4.1	−0.7
20.9	32.3	56.5	21.8	20.3	23.4	27.5
16.7	9.6	16.7	16.1	17.6	20.9	14.4
45.2	27.4 (86)	45.3 (84)	54.0 (86)	..	47.8 (86)	37.6 (81)
39.3 (86)	31.3 (86)	54.1 (84)	52.8 (86)	..	56.5 (86)	33.3 (81)
0.35	0.31	0.10	0.98	0.26	1.09	0.08
7 543	7 623	8 694	7 461	6 236	8 155	4 167
355 (84)	221 (83)	439 (87)	341	455	382 (86)	135 (82)
448 (84)	535 (83)	425 (86)	410 (86)	646	622 (84)	166 (83)
244 (84)	250 (80)	336 (83)	317 (86)	291	346 (86)	140 (80)
3.6 (82)	1.3 (82)	1.9 (86)	2.2 (84)	2.4	2.2	1.8 (82)
10.9	5.9 (84)	9.0	9.6 (86)	10.8	8.5 (86)	17.8
10.5	2.6	..	2.3	7.4	10.2	17.9
7.6	1.1	2.2	1.3	12.6	7.0	17.2
116 004	230 220	..[8]	92 592	7 164	21 804	9 144
15.4	9.7	..	43.1	20.1	26.2	25.3
9.6	12.1	..	6.9	3.4	4.4	17.0
124 596	150 300	..	91 068	7 224	22 428	13 248
16.6	6.3	..	42.4	20.2	27.0	36.7
7.7	2.8	..	7.2	4.6	7.8	6.9
23 631	57 925	..	12 818	2 298	10 105	3 047
2.7	5.5	..	2.0	4.5	6.4	3.3

BASIC STATISTICS: INTERNATIONAL COMPAR

	Belgium	Canada	Denmark	Finland	France	Germany	Greece	Iceland	Ireland
	9 868	25 803	5 130	4 932	55 627	61 149	9 998	245	3 542
	324	3	119	15	102	246	76	2	50
	0.0	1.0	0.1	0.4	0.4	0.0	0.7	1.0	0.8
	3 645 (86)	11 954	2 630 (86)	2 414	20 988	25 456	3 601 (86)	117 (86)	1 068 (86
	2.9	4.9	5.9	10.4	7.1	5.2	28.5	10.3	15.7
	29.7	25.3	28.2	31.2	30.8	40.5	28.1	36.8	28.7
	67.4	69.8	65.9	58.4	62.1	54.3	43.4	53.0	55.5
	138.9	410.9	101.3	89.5	879.9	1 117.8	47.2	5.3	29.4
	14 071	16 019	19 750	18 151	15 818	18 280	4 719	21 813	8 297
	116.5	444.5	68.4	63.3	712.2	814.7	63.6	3.8	26.7
	11 802	17 211	13 329	12 838	12 803	13 323	6 363	15 508	7 541
	1.5	4.2	2.7	3.2	1.6	2.1	1.4	3.1	1.8
	16.3	21.0	18.8	23.5	19.4	19.4	17.4	18.8	17.4
	7.0 (86)	6.9 (86)	7.8	9.7	8.3	8.4	7.1	6.5	9.4 (86
	3.4	6.4 (86)	4.4	55	5.2	5.2	4.6	3.5	4.6 (86
	2.0	4.8	6.5	1.9	0.6	1.8	-2.2	1.8	-3.7
	17.6	18.8	15.5	22.5	19.6	23.9	14.7	15.2	18.6
	16.3	19.5	25.4	20.7	19.1	19.8	19.5	17.7	18.0
	51.6 (86)	43.3 (86)	53.4 (86)	38.2	48.4	43.0 (86)	42.9 (86)	27.3 (86)	49.2 (84
	45.0 (86)	39.4 (86)	58.0 (86)	39.6	49.4	44.9 (86)	36.6 (86)	32.1 (86)	43.3 (84
	0.49	0.47	0.88	0.50	0.74	0.39	. .	0.05	0.20
	7 593	10 059	7 236	6 966	7 796	7 374	4 273	9 930 *	4 378
	335 (84)	421 (82)	293	329 (86)	369 (86)	441 (86)	127	431	206 (83
	414 (83)	664 (83)	783	615	614 (86)	641 (86)	373	525 (83)	235 (83
	303 (84)	471 (80)	392	370 (86)	394 (86)	377 (86)	158 (80)	303	181 (80
	2.8 (84)	1.8 (82)	2.5 (84)	2.3 (86)	2.3 (86)	2.5 (84)	2.8 (83)	2.4 (84)	1.3 (82
	9.4	9.1 (83)	7.9	5.8 (86)	7.0 (86)	9.1	14.1	5.7	8.9
	3.4	3.6	6.1	8.5	6.4	3.6	17.4	. .	8.8
	3.5	4.2	4.7	5.0	4.7	1.1	19.3	25.7	5.2
	2 824 [7]	94 320	25 632	19 404	147 936	293 424	6 516	1 368	15 948
	59.8	22.8	25.3	22.1	16.8	26.2	13.9	25.8	54.8
	9.6	6.5	11.1	8.2	9.0	10.7	8.7	13.7	14.6
	2 992 [7]	87 528	25 452	18 828	153 204	227 916	13 116	1 584	13 620
	59.9	21.1	25.1	21.4	17.4	20.4	27.9	29.9	46.8
	7.4	9.7	8.8	7.0	6.7	6.5	5.6	10.8	5.9
	7 958 [7]	5 778	7 153	4 592	26 161	58 846	2 007	221	3 393
	1.4	0.9	4.0	3.5	2.4	3.7	2.2	2.0	3.5

Sources:
Population and Employment: OECD *Labour Force Statistics.*
GDP, GFCF, and General Government: OECD *National Accounts.* Vol. I and OECD *Economic Outlook,*
Historical Statistics.
Indicators of living standards: Miscellaneous national publications.
Wages and Prices: OECD *Main Economic Indicators.*
Foreign trade: OECD *Monthly Foreign trade Statistics,* series A.
Total official reserves: IMF *International Financial Statistics.*

EMPLOYMENT OPPORTUNITIES

Economics and Statistics Department

OECD

A. **Administrator.** A number of economist positions may become available in areas such as monetary and fiscal policy, balance of payments, resource allocation, macroeconomic policy issues, short-term forecasting and country studies. *Essential* qualifications and experience: advanced university degree in economics; good knowledge of statistical methods and applied econometrics; two or three years experience in applied economic analysis; command of one of the two official languages (English and French); some knowledge of the other official language. *Desirable* qualifications and experience also include: familiarity with the economic problems and data sources of a number of Member countries; proven drafting ability; experience with the estimation, simulation and implementation of computer-based economic models.

B. **Principal Administrator.** A number of senior economist positions may become available in areas such as monetary and fiscal policy, balance of payments, resource allocation, macroeconomic policy issues, short-term forecasting and country studies. *Essential* qualifications and experience: advanced university degree in economics; extensive experience in applied economic analysis, preferably with a central bank, economics/finance ministry or institute of economic research; good knowledge of statistical methods and applied econometrics; command of one of the two official languages (English and French) and proven drafting ability; working knowledge of the other official language. *Desirable* qualifications and experience also include: experience in using economic analysis for formulating policy advice; familiarity with a number of OECD economies; experience in using econometric models.

These positions carry a basic salary from FF 202 200 or FF 249 480 (Administrator) and from FF 292 416 (Principal Administrator), supplemented by further additional allowances depending on residence and family situation.

Initial appointment will be on a two- or three-year fixed-term contract.

Vacancies are open to both male and female candidates from OECD Member countries. Applications citing reference "ECSUR", together with a detailed curriculum vitæ in English or French, should be sent to:

Head of Personnel
OECD
2, rue André-Pascal
75775 PARIS CEDEX 16
FRANCE

WHERE TO OBTAIN OECD PUBLICATIONS
OÙ OBTENIR LES PUBLICATIONS DE L'OCDE

ARGENTINA - ARGENTINE
Carlos Hirsch S.R.L.,
Florida 165, 4º Piso,
(Galeria Guemes) 1333 Buenos Aires
Tel. 33.1787.2391 y 30.7122

AUSTRALIA - AUSTRALIE
D.A. Book (Aust.) Pty. Ltd.
11-13 Station Street (P.O. Box 163)
Mitcham, Vic. 3132 Tel. (03) 873 4411

AUSTRIA - AUTRICHE
OECD Publications and Information Centre,
4 Simrockstrasse,
5300 Bonn (Germany) Tel. (0228) 21.60.45
Gerold & Co., Graben 31, Wien 1 Tel. 52.22.35

BELGIUM - BELGIQUE
Jean de Lannoy,
Avenue du Roi 202
B-1060 Bruxelles Tel. (02) 538.51.69

CANADA
Renouf Publishing Company Ltd
1294 Algoma Road, Ottawa, Ont. K1B 3W8
Tel: (613) 741-4333
Stores:
61 rue Sparks St., Ottawa, Ont. K1P 5R1
Tel: (613) 238-8985
211 rue Yonge St., Toronto, Ont. M5B 1M4
Tel: (416) 363-3171
Federal Publications Inc.,
301-303 King St. W.,
Toronto, Ont. M5V 1J5 Tel. (416)581-1552
Les Éditions la Liberté inc.,
3020 Chemin Sainte-Foy,
Sainte-Foy, P.Q. G1X 3V6, Tel. (418)658-3763

DENMARK - DANEMARK
Munksgaard Export and Subscription Service
35, Nørre Søgade, DK-1370 København K
Tel. +45.1.12.85.70

FINLAND - FINLANDE
Akateeminen Kirjakauppa,
Keskuskatu 1, 00100 Helsinki 10 Tel. 0.12141

FRANCE
OCDE/OECD
Mail Orders/Commandes par correspondance :
2, rue André-Pascal,
75775 Paris Cedex 16 Tel. (1) 45.24.82.00
Bookshop/Librairie : 33, rue Octave-Feuillet
75016 Paris
Tel. (1) 45.24.81.67 or/ou (1) 45.24.81.81
Librairie de l'Université,
12a, rue Nazareth,
13602 Aix-en-Provence Tel. 42.26.18.08

GERMANY - ALLEMAGNE
OECD Publications and Information Centre,
4 Simrockstrasse,
5300 Bonn Tel. (0228) 21.60.45

GREECE - GRÈCE
Librairie Kauffmann,
28, rue du Stade, 105 64 Athens Tel. 322.21.60

HONG KONG
Government Information Services,
Publications (Sales) Office,
Information Services Department
No. 1, Battery Path, Central

ICELAND - ISLANDE
Snæbjörn Jónsson & Co., h.f.,
Hafnarstræti 4 & 9,
P.O.B. 1131 - Reykjavik
Tel. 13133/14281/11936

INDIA - INDE
Oxford Book and Stationery Co.,
Scindia House, New Delhi 110001
Tel. 331.5896/5308
17 Park St., Calcutta 700016 Tel. 240832

INDONESIA - INDONÉSIE
Pdii-Lipi, P.O. Box 3065/JKT.Jakarta
Tel. 583467

IRELAND - IRLANDE
TDC Publishers - Library Suppliers,
12 North Frederick Street, Dublin 1
Tel. 744835-749677

ITALY - ITALIE
Libreria Commissionaria Sansoni,
Via Benedetto Fortini 120/10,
Casella Post. 552
50125 Firenze Tel. 055/645415
Via Bartolini 29, 20155 Milano Tel. 365083
La diffusione delle pubblicazioni OCSE viene
assicurata dalle principali librerie ed anche da :
Editrice e Libreria Herder,
Piazza Montecitorio 120, 00186 Roma
Tel. 6794628
Libreria Hœpli,
Via Hœpli 5, 20121 Milano Tel. 865446
Libreria Scientifica
Dott. Lucio de Biasio "Aeiou"
Via Meravigli 16, 20123 Milano Tel. 807679

JAPAN - JAPON
OECD Publications and Information Centre,
Landic Akasaka Bldg., 2-3-4 Akasaka,
Minato-ku, Tokyo 107 Tel. 586.2016

KOREA - CORÉE
Kyobo Book Centre Co. Ltd.
P.O.Box: Kwang Hwa Moon 1658,
Seoul Tel. (REP) 730.78.91

LEBANON - LIBAN
Documenta Scientifica/Redico,
Edison Building, Bliss St.,
P.O.B. 5641, Beirut Tel. 354429-344425

**MALAYSIA/SINGAPORE -
MALAISIE/SINGAPOUR**
University of Malaya Co-operative Bookshop
Ltd.,
7 Lrg 51A/227A, Petaling Jaya
Malaysia Tel. 7565000/7565425
Information Publications Pte Ltd
Pei-Fu Industrial Building,
24 New Industrial Road No. 02-06
Singapore 1953 Tel. 2831786, 2831798

NETHERLANDS - PAYS-BAS
SDU Uitgeverij
Christoffel Plantijnstraat 2
Postbus 20014
2500 EA's-Gravenhage Tel. 070-789911
Voor bestellingen: Tel. 070-789880

NEW ZEALAND - NOUVELLE-ZÉLANDE
Government Printing Office Bookshops:
Auckland: Retail Bookshop, 25 Rutland Stseet,
Mail Orders, 85 Beach Road
Private Bag C.P.O.
Hamilton: Retail: Ward Street,
Mail Orders, P.O. Box 857
Wellington: Retail, Mulgrave Street, (Head
Office)
Cubacade World Trade Centre,
Mail Orders, Private Bag
Christchurch: Retail, 159 Hereford Street,
Mail Orders, Private Bag
Dunedin: Retail, Princes Street,
Mail Orders, P.O. Box 1104

NORWAY - NORVÈGE
Narvesen Info Center - NIC,
Bertrand Narvesens vei 2,
P.O.B. 6125 Etterstad, 0602 Oslo 6
Tel. (02) 67.83.10, (02) 68.40.20

PAKISTAN
Mirza Book Agency
65 Shahrah Quaid-E-Azam, Lahore 3 Tel. 66839

PHILIPPINES
I.J. Sagun Enterprises, Inc.
P.O. Box 4322 CPO Manila
Tel. 695-1946, 922-9495

PORTUGAL
Livraria Portugal, Rua do Carmo 70-74,
1117 Lisboa Codex Tel. 360582/3

**SINGAPORE/MALAYSIA -
SINGAPOUR/MALAISIE**
See "Malaysia/Singapor". Voir
« Malaisie/Singapour»

SPAIN - ESPAGNE
Mundi-Prensa Libros, S.A.,
Castelló 37, Apartado 1223, Madrid-28001
Tel. 431.33.99
Libreria Bosch, Ronda Universidad 11,
Barcelona 7 Tel. 317.53.08/317.53.58

SWEDEN - SUÈDE
AB CE Fritzes Kungl. Hovbokhandel,
Box 16356, S 103 27 STH,
Regeringsgatan 12,
DS Stockholm Tel. (08) 23.89.00
Subscription Agency/Abonnements:
Wennergren-Williams AB,
Box 30004, S104 25 Stockholm Tel. (08)54.12.00

SWITZERLAND - SUISSE
OECD Publications and Information Centre,
4 Simrockstrasse,
5300 Bonn (Germany) Tel. (0228) 21.60.45
Librairie Payot,
6 rue Grenus, 1211 Genève 11
Tel. (022) 31.89.50
Maditec S.A.
Ch. des Palettes 4
1020 - Renens/Lausanne Tel. (021) 635.08.65
United Nations Bookshop/Librairie des Nations-
Unies
Palais des Nations, 1211 - Geneva 10
Tel. 022-34-60-11 (ext. 48 72)

TAIWAN - FORMOSE
Good Faith Worldwide Int'l Co., Ltd.
9th floor, No. 118, Sec.2, Chung Hsiao E. Road
Taipei Tel. 391.7396/391.7397

THAILAND - THAILANDE
Suksit Siam Co., Ltd., 1715 Rama IV Rd.,
Samyam Bangkok 5 Tel. 2511630
INDEX Book Promotion & Service Ltd.
59/6 Soi Lang Suan, Ploenchit Road
Patjumamwan, Bangkok 10500
Tel. 250-1919, 252-1066

TURKEY - TURQUIE
Kültur Yayinlari Is-Türk Ltd. Sti.
Atatürk Bulvari No: 191/Kat. 21
Kavaklidere/Ankara Tel. 25.07.60
Dolmabahce Cad. No: 29
Besiktas/Istanbul Tel. 160.71.88

UNITED KINGDOM - ROYAUME-UNI
H.M. Stationery Office,
Postal orders only: (01)873-8483
P.O.B. 276, London SW8 5DT
Telephone orders: (01) 873-9090, or
Personal callers:
49 High Holborn, London WC1V 6HB
Branches at: Belfast, Birmingham,
Bristol, Edinburgh, Manchester

UNITED STATES - ÉTATS-UNIS
OECD Publications and Information Centre,
2001 L Street, N.W., Suite 700,
Washington, D.C. 20036 - 4095
Tel. (202) 785.6323

VENEZUELA
Libreria del Este,
Avda F. Miranda 52, Aptdo. 60337,
Edificio Galipan, Caracas 106
Tel. 951.17.05/951.23.07/951.12.97

YUGOSLAVIA - YOUGOSLAVIE
Jugoslovenska Knjiga, Knez Mihajlova 2,
P.O.B. 36, Beograd Tel. 621.992

Orders and inquiries from countries where
Distributors have not yet been appointed should be
sent to:
OECD, Publications Service, 2, rue André-Pascal,
75775 PARIS CEDEX 16.

Les commandes provenant de pays où l'OCDE n'a
pas encore désigné de distributeur doivent être
adressées à :
OCDE, Service des Publications. 2, rue André-
Pascal, 75775 PARIS CEDEX 16.

72380-1-1989

OECD PUBLICATIONS
2, rue André-Pascal
75775 PARIS CEDEX 16
No. 44637
(10 89 22 1) ISBN 92-64-13202-3
ISSN 0376-6438
•

PRINTED IN FRANCE